THE
IMMIGRANT
Living on the Cutting Edge

Barbara Zavada

outskirtspress
DENVER, COLORADO

Outskirts Press, Inc.
http://www.outskirtspress.com

ISBN: 978-1-4327-9438-5

Outskirts Press and the "OP" logo are trademarks belonging to Outskirts Press, Inc.

PRINTED IN THE UNITED STATES OF AMERICA

For Jonathan, Hayden, Amber

Acknowledgements

Barbara Pyles, my gratitude for her initial encouragement to compose this account. Thanks 'Los Alamos Writing Group' for your staunch support, just telling a story. Donna Bettencourt for expertly editing my biography to 'retain my voice.' Cari Taylor for her guidance through the Internet maze.

Contents

Preface vii

Prologue
An American Wedding a b c... 1

PART I The Beginning *19*
1 Jena 20
2 U – Boat Harbor on the Baltic 25
3 Hamburg 28
4 Eagles Nest 36
5 Peace - Years after the War - Rebuilding a new Nation 38
6 Family Reunion 42
7 Switzerland 50
8 Growing up Despite Odds a b 57

PART II A New Beginning *73*
9 Migrating to the USA 74
10 Fitting into a New Family 80
11 Rochester on Lake Ontario 86
12 Promise of a Career 93
13 A Dream is Born 97
14 Recollections of New York City a b c d 100
15 Experiencing the European Continent a b c d e........... 134

16 Settling Down 175
17 Aviation - Born to Fly a b c d e 180
18 The Soviet Union a b 200
19 A Career Takes Off a b c 211

PART III Beginning Once More....................................*227*
20 Connecticut-Family-Another Career a b c d................228
21 Traveling the USA and discovering the Southwest 246
22 Freedom to Be 251
23 Jerome Studio...254
24 Freedom to Create 256

Preface

THIS IS MY story as an immigrant. This is an account of my survival through World War II and my family's exodus from East to West Germany, the devastation of the land and its people in the after war years, just plain survival, living and existing day to day. I witnessed all this as survivor, seen through my eyes as a young child.

My father, a young physicist worked at the renown Zeiss optics in Jena, East Germany. He surely would have been forced to relocate to Russia, to work on their space programs. Instead we moved to West Germany, which enabled my father to do research in the USA with tight security. This was our family's immigration, an invitation to the promised land, the USA.

This is a story from poverty to riches. This is a story of spiritual freedom of the greatest melting pot, the United States of America. This though is not a story of vastly gained financial assets but an account in which I have been given the opportunity to pursue ultimately many goals.

This is my story, born in 1938 during WW II, about shedding the emotional shackles of my troubled and most vulnerable childhood and teenage years to finally experiencing the ultimate freedoms associated with independence. This is about setting out solo at the age eighteen for New York City, called the jungle, meaning survival of the fittest. This is about the excitement of discovering new talents and experiencing joy and freedom of creativity.

It had been five years since crossing the Atlantic Ocean on

the *SS America*, passing the Statue of Liberty and checking in on Ellis Island with my family. Then one day, walking elatedly through the asphalt jungle of New York, I decided to set in writing, this incredible challenge of survival in the old world and new found opportunities and freedom in my adopted country. This is my story of the life blood of the USA, the vigor, hard labor and selfless devotion of the immigrant. Importantly though, it shows the blessings of unique talents of these immigrants brought to the American shores.

After my naturalization May 1960 came my two-year return to Europe to study, travel, and pursue cultural associations. Upon returning to the US, I began a new phase in life - career and caring for a family. Life at its best is complex. After six decades, I finally began my autobiographical sketch. I hope to capture the past with a more mature and insightful overview.

Within the measured life span of the immigrant, important family references and history can be passed on by family members. So often these valuable family records are lost with the death of the patriarch immigrant. Later, painfully, some of these facts may be recovered. Often I hear comments, "I wished I had asked more questions of my immigrant relative," or "I wish I had listened more carefully and taken notes."

Ultimate success meant for me walking the untried solo trail. I lived a heart throbbing joyful life with just as many rain clouds for hurdles. Never will I have to say, "I wished, I had." Rather, it has been a life on the cutting edge, setting out all I had set my mind to do. For this blessing I am truly thankful.

Prologue

An American Wedding a

LOOKING OUT OF my studio windows in Castle Valley, Utah, I see the panoramic beauty that made me settle in this harsh desert solitaire. West are the steep red cliffs, rising from the valley floor 1,700 feet, partially overgrown with juniper at the lower elevation of Porcupine Rim. To the south is volcanic, cone shaped, Round Mountain with a back drop of the nearly all year snow covered peaks of the 13,000 feet La Sal Mountains. East is the local landmark, Castleton Tower Rock, a red cliff monument elegantly sculpted against the seemingly ever-blue sky. Separate cliff formations are the Priests and Nuns and Professor and students. Southeast is Parriott Mesa, a gigantic square cliff rock formation with a flat top mesa and only accessible with ropes. South are the Jelly Mountains also called the Skirts. Medium high peaked, they flare out with wide folds in various shades of lavender. Each direction displays the bright red canyon of southeastern Utah but with entirely different cliff formations. In contrast, situated within this coral formation is a well irrigated valley lush green for most of the year. Tumbleweeds dominate where the natural soil had been disturbed. After this year's abundant spring rains, cheat grasses are making a dominant comeback, reclaiming their natural territory, and hopefully will displace the tumbleweeds with its allergy causing discomforts. When temperatures climb to well above a 100° up to 123° F for weeks on end, the dried grasses will form an ochre sheet across the valley floor. Late summer fire hazards will be high.

1

THE IMMIGRANT

The Ute Indians first inhabited the valley. Some caves documented their existence on Porcupine Rim along with the strenuous native switch back trail leading up the blood red canyon. The Natives called this 'the windy valley.' It may have been the reason they did not stay. Later arrivals were the Mormon pioneers, eking out a meager existence in brutal summer heat and fierce winds that could streak up from any direction. Hippies came along with the movie industry, with many films documented along the Colorado River and in Castle Valley. The film *Geronimo*, which I saw just before my arrival to Castle Valley introduced me to its awesome canyon beauty, red cliffs and soil. Artists, writers and then the well off followed, building their mini mansions. We are now a well-integrated group of Mormons, artists and affluent part timers. This is what I call home now, tending a vineyard and two small orchards on a five-acre parcel. The stucco dwelling I use entirely as studio, where I create images of the colorful southwest and abstractions of times remembered. I live with awesome beauty and greater solitude than I thought possible to endure. The only public dwelling is a Mormon church, which is also used for our much-heated town meetings. Nearly an hours treacherously curving drive along Route 128, river road, as we locals call it, the canyon embraces the Colorado River. Our social hub is Moab, with a few thousand permanent inhabitants. When night winds howl, an echo, penetrating dwellings, solitude can brace deep pain.

There is a fair amount of turnover in our valley. As Australian neighbor Jean Wilson concedes, "they are not meant to be here." Jean made the valley her home twenty-five years ago. When she became a widow, though blessed with many long time friends, she too departed. Even coupled souls, after a short endurance of this solitude, seek out a more urban community. This solitude enhances the creative output of the artists and writers. Although I productively channel this solitude towards creativity, I need to keep a balance with social and cultural endeavors. Not all my needs are met here. Short ventures of exhibits, giving talks or workshops, take me throughout the southwestern states, I reconnect with friends, as not many venture out to this remote, off-the-beaten path retreat. Yet, ferociously, too, I protect this private cocoon.

Then there is Arroyo Seco, a valley too, but less remote, an easy thirty-minute drive south to Santa Fe. This is my part time New Mexican studio. Although I require quiet, creative time, there is Santa Fe bursting with exposure of art affairs. Twenty minutes west, ascending fragmented canyon mesas, lies remote, high embedded Los Alamos, the nuclear center and birthplace of the atom bomb. This is where I look for technical assistance. Straight north along the Rio Grande, within the villages of northern New Mexican charm, lies Taos, the art colony founded a century ago by eastern illustrators. This is still today the art center but in friendly competition with neighboring Santa Fe. In this historical and cultural wealth of Native American, Hispanic and Anglo heritage, I build a contented existence. With the most contemporary arts represented in these southwestern regions, I found most what I needed.

A call came from St. Louis, MO. My daughter Erika's wedding was forthcoming, and I was to walk her down the aisle. An immigrant's aspiration is to have one's children well educated, to take a step ahead of one's humble beginnings. We toil, we gratefully sacrifice, labor the most menial jobs with lowest pay for the joy of seeing our children step above us. Erika could be called well educated. She graduated from an elite private girl's academy, the fourth oldest private girls school in the US and the former Vanderbilt mansion in Greenwich, Connecticut. For nine years she was on a scholarship, working diligently and graduating at the top of her class. Then she went on to highly esteemed Washington University of St. Louis on full scholarship, majoring in pre-med and psychology. Shortly before graduating with still another degree in engineering, she informed me of the wedding, and I was well pleased. I was not surprised about this wedding of course. During college summer break, both Erika and John Schaefer, her fiancé, worked at St. Louis Airport for Trans World Airlines, TWA. Erika worked as interpreter, translating and assisting German tourists in distress and handling international calls. Although German was to be her specialty, she chuckled over the fact that she was called upon more often to do French translations. John ably worked as their accountant.

The romance lasted several years during their studies. The wedding was set for May 16, 1998, a week after Erika's graduation. All preparations were capably handled in St. Louis. I, the mother and mother-in-law to be, just needed to be present and walk the bride down the aisle. On the guest list was her father, Gerhard, Freiherr Grote, in short Jerry, who came from Köln, Germany, and whom I hadn't seen for fifteen years. His mother, Erika's grandmother, Sabine, Freifrau von Grote, whom I hadn't seen in eighteen years, came from Florida with twin brother Klaus and new wife. Bunny McAlpine from New Jersey was Erika's godmother, a widow, escorted by Jack, her steady beau. There were seven beautiful bridesmaids who flew in from every corner of the US. The seven groomsmen were John's life long local friends. John's huge family lived in the suburbs of St. Louis. They were third and fourth generation, German descended immigrants. A bountiful family of descendents indeed.

My preparations for the wedding consisted of a mother-of-the-bride gown, which Erika ordered for me from a magazine. She wanted to be in charge of how I looked, and I did not quarrel about the price of the gown. After all, it was the wedding of my only child. The full-length gown, empire waist, prim sleeveless with high neck but open back and of playful simple swirling skirt, with matching beige satin embroidery only on the top. Fully lined, it was of crepe-chiffon with a sheer chiffon stole. Just shy of my 60th birthday, I had started menopause. I had not realized I had gained some weight in my waist, so there was a little tightness in the fit, something unusual for me to be concerned about. I would take care of that with some exercise and walking. A friend Jean Martin-Linck of Santa Fe came to lunch at my studio to check out that special dress and accessories. She approved. "Mother-in-law should wear beige and shut up." Brief and to the point was her style, and I still try to follow suit. Since I was to travel by Jeep and trailer to the midwest, I also had an oil change and the axle greased on the 13 ft Scamp. I implored the mechanic to check everything for safety, and especially do a good grease job, as I had to be on time for the wedding to walk my daughter down the aisle. So a few days before the wedding, I departed Castle Valley and headed for Santa Fe to repack at my studio. Sometimes I left the doors open of the vehicles to organize the packing, and so a little rural creature from Utah ventured along on this trip.

The journey took me through places often traveled before, such as Tucumcari, thereafter the Texas Panhandle. I always take a long rest at the National Cowboy Hall of Fame in Oklahoma City to recharge on art and beauty. It became apparent that the little stowaway was sharing my provisions. Sometimes there were muffled noises in the back of the Jeep. I would stop and search, hoping to rescue and set it free, as I suspected it to be a little field mouse. To no avail. Left alone in a sun-drenched car, thereafter strong offensive odors would prevail for the duration of the trip - - - and years to come. It was advised that, the only way to get rid of the smell was to get a new car, and that wasn't in my budget. So I endured. Tulsa, Joplin then at last Missouri.

In the evening of the third day at dusk I approached St. Louis, elated to be close. I just turned on to the city loop North 17I, when a passenger car in the adjoining lane to my left kept pace with me and tried to get my attention by lights turned on in the interior. A man middle aged with a big grin, stark naked, was exercising his erected penis right next to his steering wheel. The lights would be turned off again and he too closely passed ahead of me. This was repeated, each time he would be getting bolder in approaching my vehicle pulling the small Scamp travel trailer, trying to force me off the road. Awesome fear gripped me. Tired from a three-day drive in a tempestuous smelling car, and I was to walk the bride down the aisle. I could not allow anything to happen to the vehicles by a high speed or a hazardous exit off the busy highway. With the trailer I needed more time to slow down and stop. Would he force me off the road? In no way did I want an accident to draw attention to myself or a disturbance of any kind to mar the merriment of the wedding. He seemed like a shark attacking again and again. Moments felt like eternity. I could not just be passive. In response, then I too turned on the interior lights, turned on the flashers and started swaying gently across the road, within my lane, so as not to cause the trailer to fishtail. This I hoped would draw attention to my predicament. The predator did not want a collision after all. A few more all too close passes, and he then disappeared in dense traffic. Numb but safe I arrived to warm hugs and an apartment full of bridesmaids, young friends and joyful chatter. Yes, thank you, I had a safe trip.

Everything was planned out for me. The first night I stayed at the apartment. All other guests stayed at a conveniently located $200-a-night hotel. Robin, the maid of honor, Erika's friend from first grade in Stamford, CT, stayed at the apartment the following nights. I would have been content to stay in my cozy 13-ft trailer that had been home to me throughout my travels of the continent, but Erika felt it wasn't appropriate for a wedding guest, especially the mother of the bride to stay in homely comfort in a scamp. All had been arranged that I would stay in the spacious home of the in-laws-to-be for the days of festivities. John's mother, Betty, step-dad Dennis, and a lively group of children from a three-year-old to teens were gracious hosts.

An American Wedding b

THE REHEARSAL WAS the following afternoon at St. Marks Lutheran Church, which was also in easy walking distance to Cheshire Inn, where following the ceremony the reception was to be held. As I was waiting in the church entrance hall, suddenly, my hand was forcefully shaken. The only word I perceived was Klaus. Indeed, there was a resemblance to Jerry, my ex-husband's twin brother, my brother-in law, Baron Klaus von Grote. We had not seen one another in eighteen years. Yes, we have all grown older. Awkward silence. "I did not recognize you, it has been so long." Klaus, the younger twin by two hours, was the more out-going of the brothers. He had met and married Maggi, beautiful, tall with jet black hair and deep blue eyes while returning to Germany. The Baroness adored Maggi, her daughter-in-law. She would to no end rave her approval. She even was a secretary, just like she had been before her marriage. While I worked in the arts, in the top percent income bracket for women in the US, this was not a big deal, since women did not earn as much, and not ready to admit, that I made several times my husbands salary, who called himself an engineer at the time. In the early seventies, one would not disclose such a salary even to family at large. Jerry had attended Klaus' wedding a couple of years earlier in Germany before we met, struggling with the trip financially. Klaus and Maggi had not come from Florida to attend our wedding in Bridgeport, Connecticut. Nor was there 'well wishing' in word or note to our marriage, nor acknowledgment to our daughter's arrival the following year. Erika's life had been devoid of Uncle Klaus. Yet he stood before me, an aged man, childless with a smallish, nondescript appearing new wife, introduced as Diane. Surprise left me speechless. In such a large wedding party there were so few people I knew.

With the eagerness of a *Feldwebel*, fieldmarshal, with an aggressive stance and handshake, the Baroness Sabine von Grote, my former mother-in-law, meeting her yellow eyes and cold stare, brusquely approached me. In her early eighties, her face slightly disfigured due to brain surgery a few years back, she looked herself, self-assured and energetic. It was either her way, or no way. "Barbara," in that same raspy voice with a smile that still could only portray a mime. Neither one of us could bridge the years. After Erika's birth, initial joy turned to gloom, when the Baroness showed her displeasure at the birth of a girl. Erika was to be her only grandchild, the only descendent of the Grote hiarchy. After silence during her grandchild's growing up years, she stood before me to partake in the wedding.

With just as much forceful demeanor, Erika's father, Baron Gerhard Grote descended upon me with a big wet kiss on the cheek. A familiar grin of a hello, denying the years of non-involvement with his daughter's life, he stooped over me, still tall at 6'4" and still handsome but more rounded. Fifteen years ago had been our last brief encounter. He had flown in from Köln, Germany, and his daughter's, the last of the Grote family branch, wedding was his absolute delight.

A friend at last. Lifelong confident, Bunny and I hugged after not having seen one another in a few years. She was eighty, slender, very attractive and always elegant, with a warm heart. She made it a lifelong habit of dressing, often outrageously extravagant. With her attentive attires and demeanor she was readily the center of attention. Though for her godchild's wedding she appeared elegantly subdued. She had one daughter, Kim, but no grandchildren. From birth she had been Erika's *fairy godmother*. Her love and care spanned Erika's young life. I was introduced to Jack, her handsome and kindly mannered beau and escort. Since becoming a widow, Bunny always sported some interesting companion. She owned several homes, but Jack bought her a townhouse in Scottsdale to escape the cold New Jersey winter months and for them to pursue their passion for golf. Theatrically she flashed her large, well-manicured hand before me, her ring finger protruding with a ruby studded ring. "Jack gave me this friendship ring, to the end-of-life friendship. I do not wish to get married again, as you know."

Erika and John were totally and joyfully occupied with their many local and out-of-state friends and family. Reverend Bannitt guided us amiably through this maze of protocol. I had been responsible for raising Erika since age four, without her father's moral support. He gave little financial support at first, and then there was no support. Having been the mainstay of her life, she had wanted me to walk her down the aisle. But now I was confronted with the fact that both her father and I were to share this honor. A wedding is to pursue a young woman's ways, and I wanted my daughter's day to be remembered happily. Her father had come from Germany and with the nobility clan present, she too wanted everyone to be happy. So the three of us maneuvered down the narrow aisle, then left the bride-to-be at the altar. I then proceeded to my assigned seat in the front row, when Bunny fiercely turned on me. "You should not have gotten pregnant right after your wedding," referring to my and Jerry's financially difficult beginning years. Having had a difficult marriage from the start, this may have been my only child. I responded, "that this had been my happiest accident, and she might otherwise not have had the opportunity to become a loving godmother." In ear-shot, seated right behind us was the Grote clan.

Following the rehearsal, we proceeded to the spacious Victorian Kramer residence in the outskirts of St. Louis. Many nimble hands had transformed the ground level of a number of rooms into a festive bridal dinner gathering. The young couple sat at a large table, joined by their bridesmaids, groomsmen and friends. The rest of us sat at beautifully decorated smaller tables. A delectable buffet was set up on the wooden patio with open bar. Gratefully I joined Bunny and Jack at a small table in a love-ly window alcove. It was time to catch up on happenings and plans. After the dinner a large cake was displayed, decorated in frosty icing with *Happy Graduation Erika*. Having just graduated a week prior, thoughtfully Betty didn't want an accomplishment like a new engineering degree to be totally overshadowed by a wedding.

I mingled with various guests. It was a cool but still humid Missouri night, and I preferred staying outdoors. Jerry had been casting glances at me. Now that I sat alone, casually listening in on young folks' lively chatter, he joined me in an adjoining comfortable white garden chair. He displayed an easy worldly manner. Yet I remembered too well that this camouflaged inner turmoil. He rattled on about his favorite subject ever since I can remember. His *mother*, now her surgery, her wonderful recov-ery, and how well preserved she still was in her early eighties. With difficulty and furrowed brows he now broached the sub-ject. "I want to thank you for having raised such a beautiful child. I wasn't there, after all, you did all the work." Silence. We both reflected. He did seem to enjoy being the father of a bright, ac-complished and very attractive young daughter. Tonight and for the weekend he was to glow in the limelight as the bride's father, and this was indeed pleasing to his senses. More relaxed, he was ready to open up some more. In a few years he expected to retire. He relished in the fact that he would be quite comfortable. Having initially worked in the USA, his retirement was to draw a pension from General Electric and of course Social Security. In Germany he also had a pension plus Social Security of a kind, and of course, investments. With that said, he abruptly departed with a comfortable smile and easy manner. I was left to contemplate the years of austerity and hardship, of making ends meet despite odds. Then my surgery on both feet, to manage for most of a year on crutches, freelance work, attend to a young child and maintain a household. Utter silence for our needs on his part.

I had helped him during our early marriage attain his master of business administration degree, paving his career, then I the wife frowned upon, with only a high school education. So ill equipped, I performed the miracle, a single immigrant mother having raised and educated the now beautifull accomplished woman, the bride.

An American Wedding c

MEANWHILE I STAYED in the very active home of the Kramers. They were a large happy family, and with the preparations for their oldest son, activities were in high gear. Living alone, I was exposed to much solitude and quiet. With my daughter being married, I should have been in command. Yet, due to location and contending with John's large family and their mutual friends, the marriage was conveniently held in St. Louis. Often in modern times, a wedding is planned and financed by the young couple themselves with generous donations. Betty, John's mother, within her family, was used to being in command and all was done capably. After a long trailer trip, adjusting to Missouri humidity, low altitude, 7000 ft down to 50 ft as my car altimeter read, and not least, change of life, I felt tired, almost despondent. Yet, I was placed in the hub of things.

On the big day of the wedding, energy flowed high. Constant phone calls and friends checking in. Everyone needed to go to the hairdresser and barber. No thank you, I would just wash my long hair and place it in a clip in the back of my nape. Nor did I want a facial, manicure, or pedicure. Betty asked my opinion about which gown she should wear. The one she wore for her oldest daughter's wedding or the gown she had just purchased. The gowns seemed similar. Both gowns were long, elegant, lacy and white, like a wedding gown. She said she looked best in white. Later I confronted Erika on this matter. In an old fashioned way I thought only the bride should wear white. "No problem," everyone knew she was the bride. Besides Betty wore the same dress to her daughter's wedding. The two younger daughters, Jenny and Annie in their early teens, looked very grown up in their long sophisticated black crepe gowns as junior bridesmaids. Diamonds glimmered everywhere. The men of the house, Dennis the stepdad, Adam in his late teens, and Michael Jerome a rambunctious three-year-old adopted black boy, were handsomely robed in tuxedos.

I saw very little of Erika. She was surrounded by her seven bridesmaids in eager attendance to make her the most beautiful bride. All her friends were her best friends, so who to pick as maid of honor? Robin, she knew since first grade and no one knew her. On those early sleepover nights, they had vowed to be each others maid of honor. Robin's parents gave elaborate birthday parties for their only daughter. Erika was possibly the only Protestant association. When we would return from the Independent Language School in Westport, where I acted as Vice President for the few years she attended there, frantic calls would await us, to hurry over. The party couldn't start until she arrived at Robin's house or a designated restaurant. The only local St. Louis bridesmaid was Esther, working on her masters degree in social work, one of the college roommates, and who was Korean. Stephanie, a fashion designer in New York City, had also been a roommate, the only one married now and to her parents delight, to a rabbi's son. Heather had just returned from Africa where she interned as anthropologist. She too was from Connecticut and a former roommate. She had formed close bonds with both Ashley and Shannon during her stay in Denver. Tracy now worked in Chicago but had been a close college friend.

All brides look beautiful as I learned at a short stint as bridal designer, and this was my daughter. Her smile always radiant, this day it could not be outdone. I longed to be close to her. I wanted to hug her, to be of assistance. Yet there were seven attentive bridesmaids jealously hovering close about her, a tight-knit ring I couldn't penetrate. There was also her father's family who had traveled a great distance whom she graciously accommodated plus the many other guests, 250 church guests with 200 participants for a sit down dinner.

No one could mistake her for the bride. I remember most her radiance, her ease with ceremony and graciously accommodating her guests. She had chosen a Scaasi gown, simplicity in

Mother and daughter Erika Grote-Schaefer,1998

itself. It was a full length white satin gown, fitted through the waist and gently flared. The fitted high bodice had intricate beadwork, extended by a wide shoulder strap and also beaded band which fitted around the neck, giving a square neckline appearance. Her long, full light brown hair was aptly swept up with large curls in back by the same hairdresser all the bridesmaids attended. The hip length vail was fastened with clips below the curls. The long train could be simply hooked up expertly for the after affair activities.

On each side of the lovely bride, vail covering her face, Jerry and I eased down the isle. As the familiar *Wedding March* sounded off, a noticeable hustle began as all 250 guests rose to their feet and simultaneously flashed their cameras. For the total trip down the isle I was blinded by the repeated flashes. So I called it easing down the isle. The handsome tall groom in his impeccable tuxedo awaited us at the altar. Out of the flashes, hardly perceiving his face, I only sensed him as he bent down, kissed my cheek, and thanked me for his bride. As I searched for my seat in the front row, tears welled up. Life had not been a bed of roses, but I told myself that energy was better spent than on tears. So I hadn't planned on crying. Especially not, since Betty during rehearsal mentioned that at her daughter Tina's wedding her mother-in-law not only cried, but sobbed. I perceived this as a warning. The wedding ceremony had commenced. Erika's voice resounded loud and clear. John visibly emotional, tears streaming down his cheeks, trying to keeping his voice in check, endeared himself to us all. Then followed the sacred rite of Communion for the immediate bridal party of bridesmaids, groomsmen and family for those of Christian faith.

I was the last to exit the church as I had been in the front row. The last to give my heartfelt blessings to the newly married

Bridal Couple Erika and John Schaefer

couple. John greeted me with an emphatic Mom. Again my tears welled up. I just knew all would be alright. The guests now departed for the elegant reception at Sheshire Inn, just a short walking distance across the road from the church. Hesitantly I lingered at the entrance. A tall handsome figure approached me with a purposeful demeanor. Jerry, accustomed to often partaking in formal events in Germany, owned two tuxedos. For his daughter's wedding he chose the less formal tuxedo. He exemplified great self-assurance in these kind of functions. He had left his clan to obviously see me. Mute, from his height he simply

17

stared down upon me. After a long silence I ventured, "are you pleased with your new son-in-law? After all he is of German descent." With a grin and sweeping arm before my face, "Weber - Kramer - Schaefer - all the same thing." After this burst of arrogance abruptly he vanished, smug of his nobility.

Erika and John at their new home in Minneapolis, MN

PART I
The Beginning

1 Jena

JENA IS A picturesque town amid the foothills of the *Thüringer Wald*, woodlands in the province of Thueringia. Graduating with a *Diplom - Ingenieur*, a masters degree in physics from the *Fachhochschule* Frankfurt am Main, my father took his first job in Jena, his birthplace, to work as fledgling engineer at Zeiss, which manufactured world renowned optics. Interested in research of any kind, he discovered that we both entered this world in the same hospital in Jena and were born in the same room some twenty-five years apart, 1913 and 1938.

My father Paul Egon Max Weber was born prematurely. He survived with one of the lowest birth weights recorded at that time. His father, Max Willi Roselt, was a fighter pilot in World War I, who was shot down flying one of those open cockpit Fokker fighter airplanes. I recall always a Fokker model plane on display in our home. His father died at the tender age of twenty-one, three months before the birth of his only child. His mother, age nineteen, had diphtheria at the time of her pregnancy and was dying. Shortly before her death, to save the child, she had an early delivery. For a long time the infant Paul was confined to an incubator but survived.

My father spent his early years in an orphanage. Born prematurely, still not being able to talk or walk after several years in the orphanage, he wasn't easily adoptable. Some distant relative's only child, a five-year-old son, had fallen out of a five-story window and was killed. After the grief subsided, they remembered a boy of the same age in the orphanage. With great love Barbara

Weber devoted herself to her adopted son named Paul, and so I carry the name of this gracious lady.

My mother, born Johanna Ella Kühlich, was number four of a family of fourteen. She grew up in Stolp, province of *Pommern*-Pomerania or *Ostpreußen*-East Prussia. Her father, Ernst Hugo, tall, lean, fair and handsome, I do not remember. I was his first grandchild. He traveled a great deal on business, mostly to St. Petersburg in the Soviet Union. Having to care for such a large family, he was remembered as a very good provider. From each trip he would return with large amounts of food like barrels of butter, salted herrings or pickles. It always was a surprise what he returned with. During his stays at home he was a strict disciplinarian and was more feared than loved. When we came for visits, I was told, he absolutely adored me, and I could do no wrong. During dinner strict etiquette was observed. While he insisted on my sitting on his lap, I could get away with nearly anything and no one was to interfere.

My grandmother was Helene Auguste Kramm. Helene was also the middle name given to me. She grew up on a farm in the small town of Püttelkov in Mecklenburg with three other siblings, Ella, Reinhold and Henny of which she was the oldest. My grandmother was short, round, brunette, very calm and patient. She retained her long chestnut colored hair even at the age of 94 with only a few strands of grey, tied into a knot in the nape of her head. Her good humor stayed with her to the end and so did her good health.

As a young woman she was sent to Hamburg to learn a trade. Often did I hear her recount tales of the internship learning the skill of gourmet cooking at one of the city's finest hotel kitchens. Indeed she was a fine cook who passed her culinary knowledge to all of her nine daughters. One of my favorite stories was her falling in love with a young man named Hugo. The young women came from all parts of the country for their schooling and were strictly chaperoned. Each woman was given a small room in the uppermost floor of the hotel. After long hours of work they retreated to their rooms. Even with these restrictions, the young lovers became adventurous. My grandmother would let down a long rope from her window to the ground level many floors below. With great agility, Hugo climbed up this rope for their *rendezvous*. I do not recall if they got caught, but they did get married after the hotel - restaurant training and moved to Stolp.

My father was introduced to the Kühlich family and fell in love with all eight beautiful sisters. Two sisters had died at an early age of no known cause. *Tante* Lotte, the eldest, was the first to marry and took up residence in Berlin, the city she adored and never again left. My father vowed not to leave unless one of them would marry him. All siblings had learned a trade except my mother. Selflessly she devoted herself to help her mother raise the numerous offspring. She was held in awe and was loved by all. Her gift to the family was much appreciated and contributed to the family's close bonding in later years. With the major child rearing accomplished, she was ready to set out on her own. She agreed to marry the twenty-four-year old, handsome and well-educated young man.

My father was not very tall, of slender athletic build, very fair with light blond wavy hair, dark blue eyes with a bespectacled intelligent gaze. He seemed to me highly intellectual and reserved. His hands were delicate as he never performed any physical labor. In younger years, in a running competition he claimed first prize for the eastern provinces of Germany. His running also set an Olympic record. Training seemed tedious to him as he much preferred to indulge in his passion for physics. He once told a story of his running prowess. In a remote village a child was close to dying and required immediate medical attention, but a doctor could not be contacted. As courier he ran a great distance at top speed to the next larger town to notify the physician. Thanks to his efforts the young boy was saved. Later he confided that helping a human being survive because of his running ability meant more than any award bestowed upon him. Nevertheless he gave up his running, which had started to bore him, and instead he went headlong into research.

My mother had only a grade school education. She was acclaimed a beautiful woman. My father would tell of his love for her summer darkened skin, long straight black hair tied into a knot, large medium blue eyes set under dark brows. She was only 5' 2" with a full round figure. She always found a way to dress attractively, favoring flower printed dresses. If she couldn't afford to buy one, she would sew one up on her foot pedaled Singer sewing machine that existed since my earliest recollection. Under my grandmother's tutelage, she became a good cook and loved entertaining and merriment. After their marriage, they set off for Jena.

Here I was born as World War II broke out. My parents were a year apart in age. Due to my father's slight frame and his poor vision, without glasses he was nearly blind, he did not qualify for the armed forces. Emotions were high with the war activities. In later years it turned out to be a paramount decision to leave Jena which was to become the German eastern zone. At wars end in this eastern zone, all scientists were evacuated to Russia to work on their space programs. Certainly my parents were not aware of this most fateful decision of journeying to what was to be known as the free western zone before the war ended.

I was a happy baby of 10 pounds and length of 21 inches. Since I didn't cry, what babies are supposed to do, I was taken for a medical checkup. The lower part of my tongue had not separated and with that taken care of I performed normally. An additional but slight heart imperfection caused some concern.

My father had obtained work in Kiel but we detoured over Berlin. *Tante* Lotte and her husband Heinz lived in Berlin, the hotbed of active warfare. I know I am too young to remember these accounts. Were they illustrated to me? There were air raids all over Germany. Especially hard hit were the major towns and industrial areas. In Berlin we were inundated with air raids one after another. Night and day and day and night. More time seemed to be spent huddled in the bomb proof bunkers and supposedly sturdy cellars than in the open air.

From the vantage point of sitting on my father's shoulders, I perceived these visions. Heat. My father was running. It was dark - night. Color - the most vivid color phenomena. The streets were burning in big open flames. The buildings were tall, of many stories and dark. But the fire came out of windows, from the roofs, engulfing the whole buildings. Light, heat and flames were now starting to spill out into the street. Reds leaping with yellows, some areas rendered in purples and blues. I felt safe, perched on his shoulders, embracing my father's head as he fled. Vibrant color, stark contrasts, hard edged and vivid with emotion all became later the insignia of my art. Paintings, drawings, perhaps from the earliest remembrances, in an abstract emotion portrayed in the most vivid color spectrum.

In Kiel I felt remote from this fiery panorama. We still spent every night in the fortress of our cellar but in the morning I would wake up in my own bed. There was a blue sky and a yellow ball dancing about it, sending warmth and happiness to all directions.

2 U – Boat Harbor on the Baltic

MY EARLIEST RECOLLECTION of my childhood goes back to Kiel where I was three or four. One does not easily recollect memories at such an early age, but these were neither normal times nor normal circumstances.

The setting took place in the road before our house. Alone, I stooped on a pile of yellow sand, totally absorbed in the task of selecting one single grain after another into a small flask from the heap. I discovered each grain had a different shade. From the vantage point of a three year old, absorbed in a closer inspection of this miracle, I discovered color. I inspected meticulously at eye level with caution, harvesting this precious matter, totally absorbed with a new understanding of this wondrous world.

I was aware of this playful yellow ball dancing in the perfectly blue sky. It was there each day, one could depend on it. Clouds, for some hours or even days in this most northern part of the country, would obscure it, but you could depend on it bouncing back, ever and ever into eternity. It was reassuring to know this yellow ball would bring warmth to these northern, often cool days. This yellow ball brought color. Everything looked brighter and happier when it showed itself to us. This yellow ball, our sun, was to be constant in my life to bring warmth, color, hope and a feeling of security. The comet or this yellow ball was for those coming years my refuge. Days were sunny and predictable. One could depend on that.

Our home was on the second floor in a beautiful brick house, thus we had many stairs to climb. The garden in front of the house had a picket fence with a small gate and there were many flowers. The garden in back of the house had a very green lawn and trees. We picked fruit from these trees and ate the berries off the bushes. The *Laube,* arbor, of fragrant roses I recall best. Vines covered it entirely, leaving just a small opening. My first recollection was enjoying lunch or some refreshments in this protective arbor. I was placed on the round garden table and my mother sat on a chair. She had long black hair, tied up in a knot in back of her head, and I remember her wearing beautiful flowered cotton dresses.

It was customary for houses to have balconies. Our balcony faced the back lawn with the trees. This is where I first recall my father. He showed me the tame little bird which would fly onto his hand, and he would feed it at our balcony. I was allowed to watch but not to touch it. My recollection of my father was that he had very light wavy hair and always wore glasses. Also I recall burying the small bird in the back yard. It was assumed that I had squeezed the bird too hard while alone on the balcony. I recall folding my hands and repeating a prayer after my father. So this was my first time folding my hands for prayer.

This seemed to be the nightly ritual. I would go to sleep in my own crib. Sirens would rouse the whole population of Kiel into quick and well practiced preparation heading for the bomb shelters. Later that night I would awaken in the cellar with my parents and neighbors. The adults were in a scurry, whispering. Then came the roar of low flying planes, followed by explosions that sounded like thunder, bombs detonating on targeted industrial plants and residential communities. We huddled close, awaiting each burst. I felt numb, but trusted in my parents — awaiting the endless seeming quiet. Our cellar was large, and we had many neighbors come for shelter since not every house had this kind of a strong and protective cellar.

This was Kiel, a major city on the Baltic Sea, which harbored the submarine fleet. The British and American Air Forces heavily bombarded this city, mostly at night. We would all spend nights in this confinement of safety until all-clear sirens were heard. These loud, shrill sirens could be heard by the whole town or maybe there were several sirens simultaneously, informing us that it was the end of the enemy attack. Then each family would return home, get sleep or just start the new day. I would awaken in my own crib to just another day of the large yellow ball steadily sending happy and comforting rays out of a perfectly blue sky.

1942, only days after our departure from Kiel to Hamburg – Rissen, our house was hit by a bomb. It burned to the ground. All perished in the cellar shelter.

3 Hamburg

HAMBURG, ANOTHER TARGET, devastatingly hard hit, was a major seaport, that was to be our home for the coming ten years. Of these early years, only memories of various bomb shelters remain. We lived in the quaint suburb of Rissen with cobble stoned roads and straw thatched old *Fachwerk* homes, intricately constructed with wooden beams and brick. There were strategic plants nearby, so we were under heavy bomb attacks, again keeping to the nightly ritual of Kiel. This time our home was more modest, without a bomb shelter. The nightly exodus was to our neighbor's cellar. A number of families with small children crowded about in camaradic concern.

The next small town was the last railroad stop, Wedel, where my father worked for Möller Optics. Wedel was also bombed heavily. This company had some important factories. Rissen did not have factories, but the bombs fell upon us anyhow, though not as many as Wedel received. The nights of March 3 and 4, 1943, nearly the whole town burned down in heavy bombing. The center of town lay in ashes. So much of the local population was homeless, in addition to 7000 refuges relocated to this area from East Prussia and Schlesien.

In this northern climate it was cool, often overcast and even more often raining or perhaps just drizzling every single day, as I recall. The yellow ball was not dancing in the blue sky here as often. But it came out to play, sending its warmth and joy. You could depend on it.

The ritual we had observed in Kiel persisted. I still would go

Hamburg bombed with Sankt Michaelis Kirche 1943 - 45

to sleep in my own bed. The shrill, bone-chilling sirens to alert us to the air attacks sounded the same. The bombing persisted during the day but occurred more frequently at night. Again many people took shelter in our neighbor's cellar, each occupying a bunk or a chair. Most able bodied men had been called into the service. My father and our old landlord were the rare exceptions of men to stay with their families. My father's poor eyesight, nearly blind, and his frail build had kept him from the front. I recall his unusually high forehead with a widows peak crowned by soft fair hair, piercing dark blue eyes, cold as the depth of sea piercing into you, magnified by strong lenses. His head bent over a huge desk, books and papers neatly arranged, was my earliest recollection of his activities. He was a research physicist. Older by a few months, I now perceived the sounds of the bombs crashing into the buildings and private homes. The downpour of the bombs upon their targets were detonating, shattering explosions, crashing - crumbling. Enormous fires radiated heat waves, reverberating sounds in multitudes of dropped bombs. Again the shrill, bone piercing sirens would sound after our long confinement in the damp, cold cellar. Enemy planes had departed - for a short while. Perhaps to refuel, to restock the deadly weapons, only to reconvene with a fresh crew. My father would be the first to leave the confinement of the cellar. He would check if the sky was really clear of planes. He would also assess the nearest neighborhood for damage. When he returned to us and gave his OK that it was safe, all women and children eagerly dispersed to their own homes to resume the day's activities. After these air raids, older children would comb the streets and yards for *Granatsplitter*, scraps from exploded bombs. We managed with very little sleep.

One fearful night a bomb landed with such a loud explosion that it seemed in our immediate neighborhood. It was indeed. Our small residence was missed by a couple of feet. Although the house wasn't hit, the sounding crash was enormous as the *Brandbombe*, a smaller less potent bomb, hit the wash line and sunk deep into the ground. It could have devastated our home. Men soon appeared to deactivate the deadly weapon. A large hole was left in the fertile black earth.

The yellow ball bounced back in a plane free blue sky. It

escorted us to the beach on the Elbe River, sending its warmth and comfort, as we playfully tumbled in the high salty tasting waves of this fierce stream.

Elfi, my sister, was born in these tumultuous times. My mother had gone into labor during an air raid. Valiently my father swung himself onto his bicycle and during a torment of bombings he tried to retrieve the doctor to perform the delivery. During the blinding attack, he had to turn back. He had researched the birthing, as it was his way to research everything, and now he rose to the occasion to deliver my sister successfully.

One early morning I received a large, perhaps 15" - 20" cone shaped, colorfully decorated paper container, filled with the most tempting sweets. This was my first day of school of the *Freie Hansestadt Hamburg Allgemeine Volksschule*. It was a ritual that each child started the first day with a cone of sweets. Comforted by my mother's hand and holding the treasure-filled cone with the other arm, a brown leather *Ranzen* strapped over my shoulders, I headed off towards the two story square, brick schoolhouse in the center of town. There was a large fenced in schoolyard with one very tall majestic oak tree in the center. This is where we played joyful games during recess.

One had to attend school, I understood that, though the next few days or years I cared little for it. In back of the school was a heap of earth, a large mole or hill as viewed from above. Air raids continued on Rissen with the horrid sound of sirens warning us of enemy planes. We were trained, at the sound of the siren alarm, class by class, each with a teacher, to leave the school building and quickly head for this mole, called a *Bunker*. So many children and teachers were tightly cramped into this confined area. For the first time I recalled the panic of claustrophobia. The lighting was so dim we could barely identify the person next to us. Breathing was hard, as it seemed there wasn't enough oxygen for this tightly packed group.

Due to lack of space in the air raid shelter, it was decided that the students who lived in the immediate vicinity were allowed to run home as quickly as possible. I was the most slender student in my class from the start and the fastest runner. My earliest perception was that I would die during one of these air attacks. I was not particularly afraid of death. I pondered the thought of death frequently in those times, but I didn't totally understand death. When I was to die, the inevitable, I wanted to die in the nearness and comforting presence of my parents. So during the coming air raids, I chose to head for my parental shelter, although I lived much farther away than the immediate school vicinity.

I loved running, and I was quick. To my recollection this run home was the only event impregnated into my mind. I didn't make it home. We lived in one of the most charming suburbs of Hamburg. Streets were cobble stoned and quaint houses of brick, artfully beamed and with straw thatched roofs along Main Street. It was considered a good omen when storks nested on these roofs. The siren shrilled and I was allowed, without the cumbersome book satchel, to race for my parent's home. I barely made it to the intersection of Main Street and the railroad crossover. Bombs, *Brandbomben*, *Spiralbomben*, crashed down on Main Street with an intensity as never before happened in this town. The dropping of the bombs I did not perceive, I looked down on the cobblestones and just simply ran. I was in the midst of the inferno. Thunderous reverberations multiplied echoes of houses falling into themselves. Straw thatched roofs ignited instantly and helped fuel the inferno. There wasn't time for fear or feeling emotions of any kind. I needed to get off the street. On the side street, at the corner intersecting with Main Street, where two houses burned simultaneously, I simply hid in some green shrubs. The panorama so close at hand unfolded through my leafy camouflage. Heavy smoke started to envelop all and then the wildest fires reached out against the graying sky. I do not recall when the siren sounded for the end. Again, I ran and just ran to be united with my parents. I was six years old.

More than I feared the shrill sirens, which sounds still today reverberate a chilling remembrance, were the gas masks everyone was forced to wear. We were to protect ourselves wearing these masks from smoke and toxic fumes. They were of military green color, tight fit with a long sliver of rubber over the nose, clear round plastic lenses over the eyes and a strap on the back of the head. They came in children's sizes as well. Each member of the family was supplied one. My mask was not the right size as its fit seemed to strangle me and I couldn't get air. As usual my father's firm command prevailed and I had to wear one. I only remember the panic of being forced to wear one. Until this day I feel discomfort wearing anything tight, being confined to a small space or even receiving a tight embrace.

My father had plans for me. He idealized my becoming another Madame Curie, and I would work as his assistant. Only I didn't catch on to arithmetic. He would work patiently with me at first doing the equations, $1+1=2$. I still didn't catch on easily to early math. He'd be more emphatic, and I became more fearful of him. These sessions would continue behind a locked door so my mother could not interfere. With a harsh voice and brutal beatings about my head, I still could not produce the right answers. The more I was beaten, the less I could give the right answer, or no answer at all. His conclusion was that I must be retarded.

As much as I became fearful of my father's fits of anger, I

more feared for my beloved mother. Her beauty, her charm, her resonance, her skill of sewing, cooking and grace of entertaining, her motherhood was no longer adequate to my father. He seemed to demand an intellectual partner. Times were most stressful for everyone during this insane war and just to make ends meet demanded great resourcefulness. Witnessing my mother's beatings and disgraceful treatment would touch me more deeply than my own punishment. Unconsciously I then resolved that I would not ever allow any person to physically harm me.

Sometimes, not often, we would venture into Hamburg. *Hansestadt* Hamburg was a free city, not part of a province and an important harbor city at the mouth of the Elbe River. There was major commerce, importing, exporting, and shipbuilding, making it one of the largest and most important cities in Germany. It could be considered a handsome Nordic city within its two large lakes, the *Binnenalster* and the *Außenalster*, for sailing in peaceful times. Because of its size and importance, it was frequently bombed.

On these infrequent city outings my mother would plan on purchasing some necessities at Karstadt, the largest department store offering general merchandise. Karstadt, on the *Jungfernstieg,* a major avenue, was located on the *Binnenalster,* interior waterway, and one could walk along the lake and take in the town's activities.

We would take the train from Rissen, passing the few small towns of Sülldorf, Osdorf, and in Blankenese change for the train to take us directly into Hamburg's main station. I would always take a window seat, and some of those images etched themselves forever into my conscience. Very tall gray buildings next to the railroad passages. Whole streets burning in various degrees of destruction. I saw some more recently bombed multi-storied buildings with flames still leaping ferociously out of the debris. Reds and yellows. Other buildings caved in, flames subsiding. Eerie bluish - dense gray smoke, taking away ones vision, making eyes burn. Above, a hazy gray sky. Buildings and whole streets and even sections of town left to burn out. There wasn't labor or the means to fight these many fires. There wasn't enough labor for even emergency rescue. Sometimes one would spend a multitude of days and nights in the bunkers, celebrating holidays or even a birthday in it. It could take many days sometimes to look for those buried alive or dead in destroyed buildings and cellars. In one heavy night bombing in Hamburg, 60,000 people were buried.

4 Eagles Nest

THIS MUST HAVE happened about the time of my sister's birth. It was the first time I left the protective enclave of my family. I was sent to a children's retreat in Berchtesgaden, Bavaria. It was before I attended school and I remember the great desolation and of being unbearably homesick. But at this early age I gained the strength and independence to more readily withstand future separations from my parents when I went to camps.

My mother took me to the huge, now bomb shattered glass canopied train station in Hamburg, like she would repeat for future departures. This was the first and only traumatic parting experience. I was deposited into a train filled with children all about my age. With a small bag of fruit for the trip and in company of busy ladies attending to our needs, we departed south. It was winter. Coming from the northern flatlands, our attention was held by immense snow covered mountains, peaks reaching far into the ice blue sky. This was Bavaria. During the entire stay, we were imbedded in the pure white deep fairytale image of snow, unlike Hamburg, where snow was rare and never lasted long. At the end of our train ride, somehow we ascended a steep mountain and entered an isolated large building. We had traveled all day by train and now night was descending, as we were shown to our small beds in rooms throughout a mansion.

The next morning we were lead down a grand wide staircase to the main room, a rustic dwelling. A two story high ceiling covered this large banquet hall, where long tables were set side by side. The light was dim, despite windows facing the snowy Alps. A large bright recreation room or playroom with panoramic windows also faced the Alps. This is where we were to spend most of our time.

Deep pain of loss and homesickness obliterated my total outlook for the immediate time to follow. I begged the caretakers to mail a letter to my parents to come and fetch me quick. I was reassured that that was done, but no one came to fetch me. I insisted another letter be sent home, but this still didn't bring results and the understanding became clear - no one was to come for me. Gradually I assimilated with our small group.

There were no sirens here to alert us to air attacks. There were no low flying enemy planes in the crisp blue sky. No attacks, not even a cellar or bunker was here. We slept all night in our own beds. At least once I remember men coming, in uniforms, sitting at the tables with us children and uniformed men intermingled. At dinner, an officer at the head of the table asked me to sit near him.

There were the ever present, snow covered mountains in the near distance. We played in the confined area near the house in the abundant deep fluffy snow. The yellow ball had followed to skip between the mountain peaks. It did bring peace but not much warmth.

So many years later I learned that this had been Adolf Hitler's Obersalzberg - Berchtesgaden retreat. Many social and political functions had taken place here. He was known to maintain friendly associations with children. April 25, 1945, the American Air Force bombed the Berchtesgaden Berghoff, to total destruction. Hitler died May 1, 1945, with Eva and *Wolfshündin*, female shepherd (dog) named Blondie. Hitler and his companion Eva Braun were married in the last hour, then took their own lives in his private bunker in Berlin.

Of the Berghoff retreat the only remains are the Kehlstein Eagles Nest - Tea House.

Finally the war ended May 13, 1945.

5 Peace - Years after the War - Rebuilding a new Nation

ONE MORNING I stood behind our small home in Rissen, alone. It was spring of 1945. I was seven years old. The adults had been talking about peace. I had stepped outside. What was the meaning of that word? As I was contemplating about the changes it would bring into our lives, I glanced into the sky. In the perfectly blue sky, the ever faithful yellow ball put on a warm smile for me. There were no enemy planes in sight, geared for attack. No planes at all. There would be no more desperate escapes to our neighbor's cellar. No more bombing attacks. PEACE! Once again a *German* was allowed to think for himself. Under a dictators rule, decisions and thoughts were not one's own.

Germany had lost the war. The land was totally devastated. The Allied Forces each occupied one of the four divided zones of the country. Jena, where I was born, and Stolp where my grandparents still lived with their youngest son Jürgen, was to be the Russian zone. Berlin, where my mother's oldest sister Charlotte, *Tante* Lotte with family and another brother Ernst lived, was to be the French zone. The rest of my mother's sisters lived in Bavaria, the southern part, occupied by the Americans. We in Hamburg, the northern part, were under British jurisdiction. *Konrad Adenauer* was the first chancellor of the new German democracy.

British soldiers in uniform came even to our small, distant village. They looked content and well nourished. My father had taken me for exploratory hikes into the deep, dark forests, thick with underbrush, which started right by our house. He had taught me about plants and berries and how to pick edible mushrooms. Most of all I learned to appreciate and love nature. Immediately after the war, the soldiers came to cut down our tall trees, pines, oaks, *Buchen*. birches. Whole woods would eventually be cut down. One after another the magnificent wooded treasures would disappear, until only fields of short shrubs remained. The British Isles were sparsely wooded, and wood for manufacturing and heating was in high demand in these after war years. Trucks and gasoline were sparse, so elephants were brought in to do the labor of hauling those immense tree trunks to the nearest rail wagons, just down the road from us. I cried for our beloved and now disappearing woods. The awesome, huge, gray elephants, plodded back and forth at what appeared a slow, temperate pace, with their heavy loads, trunks wrapped around the diameter of a tree trunk, on *Höhnerkamp,* our street. We children felt the circus had come to our very own neighborhood, and we were a most attentive audience.

A playmate had lost an arm due to being buried and hurt in her burned house during an air attack. I intently studied her remaining stub of an arm while she held on to her doll with her left arm. Matter of factly she responded to my unasked question, "Someday I will only need one arm to hold my baby."

Again my mother and I, now in peacetime, headed into Hamburg. *Mutti*, mommy, was going shopping at Karstadt. From the train window seat, I could see our further remote suburbs still looked relatively sedate and calm. Once we got into the city, total devastation presented a grim gray picture. It appeared that practically all of Hamburg, the major harbor city, had burned. 35,000 had died in the city, 125,000 were wounded with 79%

of housing damaged and 49% totally destroyed. No open fires remained, but I saw some smoldering piles fallen debris, what once were *Hochhäuser,* highrise flats. Where do all these people live now I thought?

Within the country 75% of train depots were destroyed. I loved the excitement of the main terminal rail station in Hamburg, which miraculously remained unharmed except for all glass shattered in the side partitions and some in the roof. Cold drafts perennially blew through unhindered. A flood of gray masses purposefully rushed in every which direction, and the loudspeaker would emphatically announce continuous arrivals and departures for various parts of the country.

Leaving the rail station, my mother and I now walked the burned down streets still smoldering but lifeless with what once were fine settlements of solid masses of nineteenth century buildings. The fortunate survivors looked haggard and pale. People were walking everywhere dressed in muted, old shabby clothing. People in rags were begging every where. People were hungry and did not know where the next meal was coming from. When you sat down to a meal, you knew you would still be hungry after, never fully satisfied. No one could sleep, thinking about food. They were always preoccupied about what to eat. Children and adults died of malnutrition. Winters took an extra toll as thousands froze to death. Adding to this was the multitude of arrivals, *Heimatvertriebene,* those expelled from their homeland, homeless from Schlesien and the Eastern zone, needing to be housed and fed. We arrived at the Alster adjacent to Karstadt. We witnessed more people in great distress. Soldiers had returned from the front, mutilated. Men, lucky enough to return, had arms, legs or all limbs missing. There were no jobs, no income. People were begging from a populace that had nothing to give.

My father's tirades increased. I feared for my mother. I feared for myself. My parents finally divorced. I felt soothing calm and quiet released from the family trauma. In school we were inoculated again and again. Diseases were rampant and took lives. Doctors and nurses gave checkups to whole classes at a time as we each stripped our upper torsos. From the start I had been the most slender and frail in my class. Meals consisted of a thin soup or a slice of cornbread, which I roasted on top of the small coal burning stove. So now our parents were informed that the children in fear of survival and in most desperate jeopardy were to be send to camps *Erholungsfürsorge* for special nurishment and care to our neighboring and nutral country during war, Switzerland.

6 Family Reunion

EAST GERMANY WAS now under Russian jurisdiction. Russian soldiers penetrated and plundered the land and shipped everything back home. This was the custom of defeated lands from earliest Old Testament days. My grandmother Helene, and her youngest son Jürgen, about age 13 or 14, buried valuables deep down in the ground near berry bushes in the vegetable garden before this

Grandmother Helene Kühlich in her youth

invasion. This practice, was common but easily detected by soldiers testing the soil with long swords.

In *Stolp,* now renamed Slupsk in *Pommerania*, the last train ride to West Germany and freedom was announced spring 1945. Families packed up time treasured belongings in small hand held parcels wildly scrambling for the last exodus to freedom. Ten million refugees were in flight and in need of shelter. At this time my grandfather was gravely ill. As my grandmother recalled, he had lost all sensitivity in his legs, was bedridden, and gradual numbness advanced toward his heart. He urgently persuaded my grandmother to take advantage of the last train ride west without him, as he felt he would surely die soon. But my grandmother's decision was to stay behind and care for her dying husband. Shortly therafter she and Jürgen buried him. Meanwhile her second oldest daughter, Ilse, had miraculously and under many hazards arrived in Stolp to escort her mother and young brother west.

Many years later I met Irmgard Macke, who's husband had been missing in Siberia towards the end of war. Irmgard confided, every night the Russian soldiers took my older sister and gang raped her, and in the morning she would be returned. Their mother tried to hide her daughter, but the soldiers always found her. One morning she was found dead on their homes doorstep. She was twenty-five years old.

Irmgard came from the Polish corridor, a narrow neck of territory separating East and West Prussia from the rest of Germany. It was territory lost after WWI in 1918. In 1938 Hitler was trying to reunite the provinces. This was the cause of the invasion of Poland in 1939. With no preparations, Irmgard, with her young children was able to take this last three-day train ride in an open top, animal wagon. Sixty adults and children were crowded in with the latrine in one corner, offering no privacy. As the train chugged down the tracks, the refugees hunched on the wooden floor. With nothing to eat, many froze to death. At night three inches of snow blanketed them. A young mother embraced her two dead children.

Those who stayed behind were called the 'war brides'. *Volksdeutsche,* ethnic German, were made the *Sündenblock.* scapegoats. Girls and women ages 18 to 30, were ripped out of their beds at night and were transported in animal wagons to Russia. Expelled to forced labor, with little food, many died. Irmgard spoke in a tearful soft voice. Today we are forgotten. No one has heard of those transgressions against us. There has been no compensation. We lost everything. There was no return. At the borders we were shot. In Germany we were refugees. In 1989 the borders between East and West were opened. Today we are free, but we no longer have families.

Grandmother Kühlich with some of her children.
Left Ilse, Gerda, Alice - Grandmother, my mother Johanna, Ernst,
Hans, Asta, Lotte, Ruth, 1930

Of those not having made the last train, small groups banded together to attempt an exodus on foot from the most Eastern section of the province, Stolp, close to the Polish border, destination Berlin - West Berlin. The town of Stolp no longer exists under that name. From time eternal, borders had been moved and towns renamed.

My grandmother, well advanced in years, having born fourteen children, a dozen still alive, and not in best of health, was among them. Malnutrition and diseases were rampant. So each person prepared for this momentous and uncertain endeavor of a journey with a hand carried parcel or shoulder bag filled with necessities. After deprivations of a long war there were shortages of everything. They traveled with threadbare clothing and old shoes, or when they wore out, rags wrapped about feet, not knowing where the next meal was to come from or day shelters to be found. The exodus for survival on foot was managed by night so as to stay undetected from Russian authorities. The Eastern sector still needed to be worked and managed by labor, so departure for the West had become illegal, especially for the young and those with professional skills. Now before dawn each morning the intimate group searched for not easily detected shelter to rest up for the coming night walk. Shelters often were bombed out buildings or abandoned farms and residences. Sometimes they stayed in the thickets of the woods, and more rarely, they were sheltered by sympathetic kin folks who themselves were forced to remain.

The long nightly marches proved treacherously hard on my grandmother's already ailing feet. The only pair of already worn out shoes gave out. My grandmother's feet were bound in cloth for the rest of the journey. Russian soldiers did detect the small group numerous times. Their small parcels of belongings plundered long ago. They forged on. Young attractive daughter Ilse was repeatedly raped by whole groups of Russian soldiers. Again, this is the fate of women of defeated lands dating to ageless times. As they could not return, only the thought of their family already in the West expecting them gave them iron courage to proceed. How long did this trip take? I do not recall. Many weeks or best, many moons.

Benevolent aid at times, when severely physically and emotionally beaten, rekindled their spirit. After long deprivations they did arrive in Berlin. Jürgen, the young teenager, best survived this exodus. Reaching their destination, both my grandmother and Ilse immediately had to be hospitalized. With doctors care my grandmother's severe exhaustion and injured feet were treated. She had never been that trim. Ilse stayed longest in hospital care for her internal damages due to repeated rapes and toll of exhaustion. Yet during that treacherous journey, she continued to guide and protect her family to bring them safely to their destination, West.

After the war Irmgard was reunited with her husband. He had survived Siberia in severest hardship with 50° below Fahrenheit. In Stalingrad he had been buried three days but survived. Of 700,000 soldiers, only 100,000 returned.

Lotte, an older daughter, provided temporary accommodations to the refugees. She took great pride in her modern and beautifully decorated apartment. Although she, husband Heinz, and young daughter Brigitte had the most space and comfort to offer, food was most sparse everywhere, so she encouraged her family to proceed north to my mother's home.

So it happened that the refugees came to Hamburg - Rissen and to my mother's genuinely warm welcome. After my parents divorce, my father had taken his separate quarters but still came to visit Elfi and myself. We lived in a small stucco dwelling, a *Hinterhaus*. behind the elegant two story home of the Bohn's on Hönerkamp. We rented the place, which was attached to the pigsty. Possibly the whole dwelling could have been a pig pen at one time. One or two pigs stayed in that pen as long as we lived there, rummaging around at night, perceivable to us in our adjacent sleeping quarters. The house consisted of a kitchen with pantry on cement floor. There was a big black stove, which was never used, a small gas stove and a water faucet with a small white sink. There was a kitchen table with pullout that contained two washbasins, where we washed up, and it was also used for dishwashing and doing laundry. Of course there were numerous chairs and a cabinet to hold dishes.

The living room had a brown and beige patterned cocosmat rug, a small round coal burning stove, a couch my mother slept on and a table with chairs, which I recall always being occupied by the various family members staying short or longer term. The only bedroom held the arriving multitude. Elfi was safe in her crib. The former parental beds were pushed together to fit into the small room, myself destined to sleep on the wooden and drafty crack between beds. I'd snuggle to the edge of one bed or the other, just be pushed back by whatever occupant onto the crack. Around the house to the back, there was the wooden shed to accommodate those who didn't fit inside. A cubicle inside with door was the outhouse. On occasion the bucket had to be emptied. As a young child I was afraid to venture into the dark, rat invested shed to the outhouse and my grandmother patiently would accompany me.

Neighbors inquisitively wondered how so many of us would fit into the small house. It was my mother's gracious hospitality and love for the siblings she helped raise, now in need, that compelled her to share the very little she had. After my return from my stay in Switzerland, I still maintained fearsome low bodyweight and continued to receive highly valued food stamps for supplement to our rations. These prized rations now contributed to feed the arriving family. I did not benefit from the rations, and so stayed dangerously underweight, but the rations kept coming. Refugees now included Oma, Jürgen, Ernst, Ilse, Ruth and daughter Marion with various other family members frequently wanting to visit with their mother.

These were the darkest days. My mother obtained a job at a Lucky Strike cigarette factory, commuting by train to Hamburg, as she had remained the only one of her family uneducated and not skilled in any profession. Selflessly she not only helped raise her siblings but now she housed and supported them as well, the life giving family branch to support their eventual independence.

Theft was common. One could not leave laundry drying outside on the line, unwatched, especially at night. No one could afford to loose the little clothes one possessed. My mother took some of the cigarettes that she tended on the assembly line. She put them beneath the sole inlay of her shoes. Cigarettes, even squatted down flat, were a treasure. With inflation out of hand, cigarettes were highly valued in trade. She bartered with them for coals and briquettes to kindle our small stove, which we all huddled close to during those most freezing winters one remembered after the war. The living room was the only room heated. With sparse heating materials, one would go to bed early and tuck into the feather quilt. Bricks could be warmed on or inside the stove, then wrapped in newspaper and taken to bed to warm our feet. The bedroom walls with no insulation had a faint sheet of frost to the touch of a bare hand, balls of ice would swell over nails beneath the wallpaper. Windows displayed the most beautiful patterns of abstract frosted flowers with no occasion to melt.

So at night, when the trains pulled into Rissen railroad station, just down our street Höhnerkamp, less than half a block from our house, my mother set out to negotiate carrying a small sack. She was a beautiful brunette in her early thirties, with an attractive figure, and with charm I'm sure, she met the train conductor or engineer to trade her crushed cigarettes for a supply of coals that were meant to run the steam engine. Only she could pull this off. No one else in the family would bring in supplies. My mother also bartered for food by mending and sewing new items since she showed a special skill for this. At times we went to *das Alte Land*. The fertile land lay beyond the Elbe River, and I was allowed to join and help carry the acquired goods. It was a long walk to the Elbe River, where we then enjoyed a ferry crossing over the turbulent stream with unknown multitudes of live mines not yet detonated. A high dam protected luscious fertile land well below sea level. So my mother and I descended the dam and now faced a road of stately and beautifully painted *Fachwerkhäuser* of the fruit farms. Purposefully she approached the farmers to negotiate to trade for potatoes, bread, dairy products or fruit. Often joyously we returned home to our hungry family. She was indeed the provider her father had once been to his large family.

7 Switzerland

IN SCHOOL IN 1945 we were inoculated again and again. Diseases were rampant and took lives. Doctors and nurses gave checkups to whole classes at a time as we each stripped our upper torsos. From the start I had been the most slender and frail in my class. Meals consisted of a thin soup and a slice of either *Mais* or *Roggenbrot,* which I roasted on top of our small coal-burning stove. We rarely ate potatoes but there were abundant *Steckrüben,* turnips or sugar beets. So now our parents were informed that the children in fear of survival and in most desperate jeopardy were to be sent to camps *Erholungsfürsorge* for special nourishment and care to our neighboring and neutral country during war, Switzerland.

In my school and the town of Rissen I was the only child selected for this humanitarian act for survival. My mother seemed to be delighted about this good turn of events. A several month stay with a family in Switzerland was planned for this small group of children. Happy emotions were quickly dampened as we were notified of yet other health screenings in Hamburg, when many children were again and again eliminated from this program. Children chosen to live with an individual Swiss family were few and carefully screened. All parents most eagerly wanted their children to be selected. At the last checkup I felt almost faint with anticipation, so much did I, so much did all the children and their families, want to be finalists. Once more I bared my upper body, every rib sharply protruding, skin close to the bones and joints, breathing softly. My neck was very long and skinny above a small head. Facial skin taut over the protruding cheekbones. In this small face were burning eyes, large deep blue eyes. My skin and hair color was the fairest. I was pronounced the recipient - the few of so many hopeful and needy anticipants. My mother wept. As we departed, disheartened parents sat on benches, crying for their children who had not been accepted.

The children selected in what was now West Germany were few. The several months stay required minimal preparations as we set out for Hamburg - Hauptbahnhof, where again my mother deposited me on a train. At seven, a few years more mature, and having experienced the previous parting for Berchtesgaden, I was better able to withstand this long separation. After a considerable train journey, we all got herded into a preparatory camp of short stay. Then we were dispersed to our individual host families after yet another long train ride.

What seemed like a very long ride, I was taken to the farm country in the outskirts of Zurich. Family Merkt lived on a small farm in a community with only a few other farms and inhabitants. The kindly couple in my tender youth seemed old. With already a grown daughter working at a local out of town factory, which produced straw baskets and objects of kind. Martha always sported an encouraging warm smile and wore long colorful embroidered skirts, white blouses, the local *Tracht*. Bruno, their young son was just a year or two older than I. He seemed sturdy, solid, with dark brown hair and clear bluish-green eyes, and yes, he was mischievous. We were to become companions in mischief. On the upper floor, under the roof, walls slanted, for the first time I had a room of my own. I only slept there, as life on a farm was busy with many chores.

The farmhouse with its numerous small rooms and the adjacent barn was very old. The kitchen seemed antique and dark with its wooden cupboards, sideboard and pantry. In the main room we had our meals on the small but adequate wooden table, with a chair for each of us. The raw wooden floor had a magnificent *Kacheloven*, oven entirely in green tiles. A wooden bench skirted around the oven and way on top near the ceiling were stored during summer months the giant bottles of home made vinegar, also where one could hide out undetected. A small window radiated light through the abundant geraniums in the outside flower box. An earth-floored basement stored the preserves, the barrels of apple cider, wine and the huge, infrequently home baked round loaves of dark rye bread. One ascended the home by a wooden stairway with aromatic red geraniums arranged along one side of each step.

There was a fierce barking black watchdog tied to a chain near the back kitchen entrance. One of the first acts was to become acquainted with Wolf by taking him his bowl of daily rations. Bruno seemed fearless but not affectionate towards the dog. I lost some fear but nevertheless stayed clear of the reach of the dog chain. In the barn, attached to the dwelling, the cows were milked, a chore Bruno and I helped out with. During milking, once a cows tail disengaged itself from the restricting wire line it was tied to. It slapped me hard clear across the face with fresh dung from its furry tail. I do not recall milking since that incident. The rest of the barn was used for storing hay. Pigs were kept in a separate stall. Feeding them were also chores Bruno and I shared. Of course there were many chickens pecking about the yard and a rooster to awaken us mornings. The family had a good amount of beehives. The bees were plentiful in the apple orchards, often not easily detected near the half-wasted *Fallobst* - grounded apples. Bruno and I mostly walked barefoot except when going to church on Sundays. We both got the bottoms of our feet stung many times, but Bruno seemed the hardier and did not require the care of vinegar rubbed to the sores.

We had abundant food. Meals at our comfortable small wooden table in the main room were a meeting and resting occasion from chores. I remember the most tasty, fragrant soups with vegetables and things I couldn't identify. The home baked dark rye bread was the best I'd tasted, and one was allowed to eat more than one slice. With it was abundant homemade butter and cheese or honey. During the day we snacked on apples, pears, plums on branches in reach, gooseberries, red and black *Johannesbeeren*, currants from the vegetable and flower garden.

Amazingly, I was asked whether I wished to attend school. Politely I accepted. Then, what would have been in store for me without my companion? Surely more chores. The red tiled roof stucco building had two rooms. Bruno and I stayed in the room with first to fourth graders, one teacher to a room, each schooling four classes. Students sat in single rows for each grade, one student behind the other. For the first time school seemed easy. Coming from a Hamburg suburb school, we were much advanced. Bruno struggled hard. I too struggled comprehending my first foreign language, *Switzer Deutsch*. No one spoke high German, but at that tender age, I quickly absorbed what I needed to converse with the family and at school.

Martha and mother Merkt taught me to knit. I knit wash cloths in pastel colors in fine cotton yarn. I did not take to knitting easily and so it was used as a form of punishment. I could be taken for a tomboy, loving the outdoors, and I remember a lot of time sitting in the main room in a corner on a little chair knitting the wash cloths. One time hiding on top of the green tile oven behind the vinegar bottles, jumping from my hideaway, my skirt got caught on a bottleneck of the homemade vinegar. The gallon bottle fell, broke and the precious commodity spilled. Bruno and I took turns with chores and special punishment chores. We swept the entrance stairs, lifting each of the many geranium pots. Feeding the animals. Churning butter in the ceramic crock with the long wooden handle was hard work and tedious. Bruno was more energetic and adept in this chore.

A visitor arrived for an afternoon, another German girl, Kate of my age, seven, who stayed at a nearby town. No chores that day. We played. I showed her about the farm and introduced her to the animals. I gave her food for Wolf so she could make friends with him. She was a city person and not familiar with watch-dogs. During that afternoon she got into Wolf's domain within his chain range and he took a hearty bite into her buttocks. As Kate was my visitor, I was held responsible. Wolf's teeth marks showed bloodstains and I felt deeply sorry. Kate never returned.

The only occasion for us children to wear shoes was going to church. I do not recollect attending church but a few times. Church was a long way off to the nearest town and Bruno knew the way along long stretches of quiet country roads. The adults I suppose had to uphold the farm, take care of the animals so Bruno and I could attend the worship. The bell in the steeple of the small stucco church building could be heard from afar and welcomed us after our long walk. Details of the service are for-gotten, only the spirit of that experience is remembered.

There were frequent school closings. In this remote rural farmland community all the help was needed during harvesting. Too well I remember the potato harvest in the brutal heat of late summer. We followed the bare furrows, exposed by the oxen pulled plow, barefoot of course. The potatoes were gathered and deposited at the end of the rows. It was hard physical work and generous snacks of Helvetica foiled cheese was distributed without bread to energize this small team. The Merkts were nearly self sufficient I observed.

School exemptions were also observed for apple harvesting and the frolicking times of cidering with the communal cider press when the whole village participated. Fresh pressed apple cider, just served from the press was at its best and spirits ran high. High time activity was also harvesting luscious white grapes from the vineyards beyond the hill of the house. We cut grapes and deposited them into our small baskets. Our filled baskets then were emptied into a large basket container with shoulder straps. When full, it was strapped to a man's back and then heaved onto the waiting wagons pulled by oxen. Most of all I recall this festival, following the grape harvest. We dressed up in our finest, wore shoes. There was singing and dancing, carefree joy from hard labor. Relaxation and partying lasted late into the night. We children were free to experience and explore the merriment into the morning hours when each family returned to their homestead by wagon.

This enlightening experience of my early years came to an end after harvesting when cooler weather approached. I was allowed to take home one of the much labored over, hand knit wash cloths. A bright red, front-buttoned warm sweater and hat with intricate white wool design in the back of the head were specifically machine knit for me. Happily I snuggled into the outfit for my departure, leaving a loving foster family to return home to my family in Hamburg - Rissen.

I had never totally fit into the northern German community, although arriving at a young age. My family spoke the East German dialect of *Ostpreußen* - Prussia. Consequently I too picked up this discerning speech pattern. After my many month's of exposure to *Switzer Deutsch,* my speech now was fragmented of that tongue as I groped back into high - German. Every one delighted in my speech and I was repeatedly encouraged to talk in school and wherever I turned. Almost immediately the beautiful red hat, earning me the name *Rotkäppchen* - red riding hood, were stolen from me. The warm red sweater, which was to last many seasons, too, almost immediately disappeared. Those were the most difficult years to endure right after the war and there were frequent thefts. Yet I could never be severed from those warm memories of my stay in Switzerland.

8 Growing up Despite Odds a

MY FATHER HAD taken up a partnership of scientific research with Dr. Fröngel. The laboratory was stationed in Fröngel's villa in Rissen's outskirts among tall pines, *Fischteichen,* and within walking distance of the beautiful heather country. My father now worked full-time on research. With an assistant he set up his workstation in the mellow and luscious flat meadows in the vicinity of Wedel. There was a rustic shed to house some of the vibrating, flickering and ticking devices interconnected with a maze of wiring. I was invited to be present but not to touch. After a few electric shocks, like a guinea pig, I learned what to stay away from. We slept in hammocks strung from the ceiling, floating above the technical paraphernalia. I had my own small fiber strung hammock with pillow and blanket. In the mornings there was fresh milk, purchased by my father from the farmer who in the early hours had just milked the black and white spotted Holstein cows peacefully grazing around us.

In the northern sector of Germany, under British jurisdiction, plundering continued. Again in my father's company, scientific equipment was hidden, possibly the Fröngel - Weber, inventions in their experimental stages. We delved deep into the forests to disperse and camouflage the equipment, all of manageable hand carrying sizes and weights. I do not recall if indeed this was recovered and by whom.

Some time prior to the end of war, my father was employed in Wedel, Holstein. He researched for *J.D. Möller Optische Werke GMBH.* Möller had ties with universally known optics of Zeiss in Jena, Thühringen, where my father originally worked. The founder was Hugo Möller, but I recalled him talking about Dr. Hans Möller, the son and heir in intimate terms. Close to the end of war, the factory was bombed and totally destroyed.

In Flensburg - Schleswig Holstein, at the most northern border, my father now set up his independent concern, situated right at the Danish border where he also patented his works in that country. He was a theorist and a research physicist, always deep in thought, showing little concern or awareness of everyday affairs. A businessman he did not profess to be. Yet he received highest accolades and respect by his peers. After remarriage to Gertrud and birth of Norbert, they moved to the mountainous Harz region. Unemployed he maintained a subsistence existence. I do remember him always bent over his desk working on formulas few of his friends or acquaintances professed to comprehend.

The perpetual visiting and needs of my mother's siblings and the hardships of providing for two young children single handedly eventually wore her down to deep depression and a breakdown. Elfi and I were left in our grandmother's care while she was sent to recover and rest in a convalescent home. Then I do recall how my mother radiated with beauty and energy when she returned after the many weeks of our separation. Additional food stamps designated for my supplemental nutrition failed to improve my weight gain and general well being as we still shared quarters and provisions with our extended family. Again after health screenings at school I was sent to a *Landverschickung* camp in the *Lüneburger Heide*, heather. With great joy I always looked forward to these camps, escaping the strangle of the tight knit family. Here I found company of children in like situations, sharing outings in the beautiful heather land I learned to love. Even here I received special rations aside from my companions. Our camp area included a small castle. We stayed in barracks but had our meals in the castle dining hall. Initially I had solitary confinement to a charming room in the castle tower with awesome views of the violet heath all about. Once I had gained some weight and improved my stamina, I was allowed to return to the barracks to mingle with the other children.

After returning home from these and other camps like *Wyck auf Föhr*, *Nordfriesische Inseln*, an island community in the North Sea, close to Denmark, with improved weight and spirit, in a short time I was in the same situation as before. Ernst and Jürgen, my mother's youngest siblings now had jobs and contributed to the household finances. My grandmother prepared fragrant smelling meals for her sons and other family members. I once asked, why do I only get fried potatoes with an occasional egg or a thin soup with noodles and am never given meat? The reply was, "your father doesn't contribute to your and Elfi's support." Occasionally I did get fish; it was more abundant close to the sea.

I became aware that I was different from my family, from my mother's family. All were physically attractive people with an aggressive outgoing personality. They were large boned with dark hair, dark skin, even darker after tanning on the Elbe beaches. Everyone dressed attractively despite hard times and rations. My height was average but I was very slender, fair of skin and hair. My temperament was different too, as I was derogatively referred to as the *dreamer*. I tried to fit in and be more sharp, but I wasn't. With a mellow mood, enjoying nature and isolation, I was happiest left to my own thoughts and pastimes.

It must have been during my mother's absence when the family descended upon me again and again to assess my looks. I had to cover my face, just eyes showing. Yes, the eyes were acceptable. Then without my hand cover, hair the color of straw, my seemingly large nose in a small plain face was ugly. I had a wide mouth and full lips not in proportion to the small face. My teeth were even and white, but were too large with an unattractive gap in the center front, claiming my smile reached from ear to ear. This ugly face rested on a neck too long and skinny. The body was so frail and thin it did not need even mentioning. Clothes were lucky enough to have consisted of hand me downs. It was agreed, as the first born grandchild, I came after my father, not a Kühlich. In comparison my cousins were not only adorable in nature and pretty, but already proving to be smarter as well. No one paid attention to my schoolwork, but at the end of each semester, I would fearfully bring home my report card for my mother's inspection and of course her signature. It became tradition, with the family in attendance and outspoken approval, that I would be severely punished by my mother with the cane rug beater.

After the beatings my mother's heart would soften some. Inspecting the report card a second time, she reflected the poor grade I received even in sport, yet my being the fastest runner and best athlete in the class. All grades were equally poor, but she enjoyed the drawings I brought from school and I had helped my friends with their sketches. In sewing and needlepoint she could attest to my meticulous and beautiful work. Thoroughly I enjoyed poetry, learning by heart long passages by Theodor Storm, Heinrich Heine, Schiller, Göthe. Reciting poetry out loud, page after page, for skill and emotion, I was at the head of my class. Herr Zühlke then made me recite other poems as well until I lost my calm, stumbled and lost first place. In arithmetic I had a hard time catching on and lingered at the bare bottom of the class. We progressed to algebra and high math for which my interest kindled. I could do no wrong. Perplexed, Herr Zühlke, our teacher in every subject except sewing, called in the much feared principal. Beatings by the principal were still common and acceptable. With the whole class in attendance, the principal somber in the back of the room, I was given formulas to equate on the blackboard with chalk in front of all. Perplexed, Herr Zühlke explained to the principal, that I had been the poorest student in arithmetic, isolated on my own, now I could do no wrong with advanced math, just like he tried to demonstrate with me on the blackboard. Herr Zühlke had come from what now was East Germany. He was tall and stout and outgoing. His wife, short and modest with two teenage daughters, joined him many years later, coming from the Eastern sector. After I departed his class to leave Germany, he was promoted to be principal of our school.

Yet young, I was not surprised of my aptitude. The family had assured me that I took after my father. I was fair, frail and I excelled in sports like him. My father was also a physicist, mathematician and poet among other things. He was intelligent, I knew that, but he was absent in my life. I could not think myself to be smart, but just maybe, I had an aptitude to be capable after all. I too was barely aware that I had a single mother, living in greatest poverty, and therefore I was awarded the lowest esteem.

My grandmother, affectionately surrounded by her many daughters and two sons was in mourning. Her eldest son Hans, my godfather, was still reported missing. He was the handsomest and the smartest of the siblings it was agreed. Early in the war he had volunteered to serve in the army. His last whereabouts was thought to be in Siberia. While we shivered in the cold with little heat in the freezing winters after the war years, we knew Siberia was colder than even perceivable to us. It was said "no one returned alive from that frozen wasteland in Siberia." Report came to us, that by the thousands soldiers froze

61

to death in the vast steppes of Siberia with inadequate clothing and ill nourished, performing slave labor. Yet true to the nature of a mother, surrounded by love, it was Hans foremost on her mind, in her talk and prayers. He was only reported missing and hope of his sure survival, somewhere in that much feared, far off Russian territory, sustained her into old age. Many years later I contacted the Red Cross in Germany regarding the whereabouts of my godfather. The painful response was that he was still considered missing, but with fair possibility perished the first days of September 1944 in Rumania.

July 11, 1944, the attempted assassination of Hitler, Himmler and Göring by Graf von Staufenberg failed. An underground group of generals and high officials formed with hate and conviction, considering him the greatest tragedy that could have happened to the German people. If Hitler indeed would have been assassinated, plans were for an immediate standstill of this insane war and recall of all troops from the fronts, including Rumania. If these plans had succeeded, Hans Joachim Kühlich, my godfather might have returned alive.

We had a radio. We listened to classical music, often opera on Sunday afternoons. We also heard the news. Winter weather temperatures were at record breaking lowest. Many people, even whole families died in their homes for lack of heat. The most devastating news reports to me was listening, for hours long, of lists of mainly children missing, names or descriptions given in hopes to be reunited with their parents and families when they were separated on the East to West exodus. Life was at its hardest, but I had a family.

My grandmother proved to be a wonderful storyteller. Times brightened with her telling of carefree days about her childhood in Mecklenburg or in Stolp raising her large family. My grandmother too was able to still recite long passages from the Bible she had to memorize as a child. So I surmise that she was the person to kindle the spirit of my faith along with encouraging prayer. Surprisingly none of her children or other grandchildren followed her faith. Often I prayed, almost always for my mother, for she seemed so deeply troubled and remote, often crying violently. I did not know how to approach my mother, to console her at those times. I just prayed that her life would lighten up.

In those downcast days of hardships, even after cloudy, rainy, depressing days, of which there were many, rays of sun, warmth and kindness trickled into my life. I had two friends who were sincere and dear to me. Gerlinde Bendix, Fridel Bröckel and I shared outings into the woods, marshes and pastures, the colorful heath or beyond to the Elbe River. Gerlinde was taller and stronger than I was, with dark curly hair knotted into long braids. She loved to smile and was ready for mischief any time. She lived in a magnificent wood block house her father had built himself for his large family. They had a large piece of property filled with an orchard of a variety of fruit trees, a vegetable and flower garden. A small herd of Heidschnucken, sheep with long fur and curled horns, grazed in the fenced in pasture. The Bendix family feasted on the Heidschnucken, and Gerlinde the youngest, bitterly complained to me, that her father always served her the smallest piece of meat. I did not think it important to mention, that I never ate meat. With so little food for human consumption, the Bendix family had a dog, a most annoying ever barking black watchdog kept on a line next to the kitchen entrance. Gerlinde always had to calm him or hold on to the animal when I came for a visit. She had a lovely family of sisters, brothers and a grumpy, very tall and frail appearing father, who often had to leave for a sanitarium for his lung ailment. Her mother was the kindest gentlest person I knew then. From the wool of the sheered sheep they raised, she'd spin yarn on her spinning wheel and then knit clothing for the whole family.

Fridel was stout, not athletic, yet we walked, but shorter distances. Her hair was red-blond and as the custom was, braided. She had a prominent hooked nose, freckles and an ever-happy smile. She lived in a small villa in the outskirts of Rissen, which had been in her family for generations. Eventually when Fridel married, her older brother having migrated to Canada, she too settled in that house to raise her family. The area was surrounded by lakes and the Elbe River. It had been our prime motivation to learn to swim at an early age. We all knew already to cross our favorite *Fischteich*, fish pond, but Fridel. Ernst had passed his life saving test, the custom for young men, and talked extensively about the life saving aspects, approaches and dangers. As the most slender, I was also the hardiest, ever running when possible, outrunning everyone, even older boys. It was time for Fridel to test herself to cross the pond. Covered with sea roses and cattails, only the center passage stayed clear of strangling vines due to swimming traffic. If Fridel grew tired, I'd promised to help her. So she set out kicking and splashing profusely and in safe distance I glided along her side. Then she panicked as she grew tired a little more than half of the crossing. I asked her to turn on her back. Safely from behind I grabbed her chin, which rested on a strong neck, lifting her head slightly, as I pulled ahead while she paddled some with her feet. Within a short distance I was able to touch ground. Both of us were even happier when she crossed the pond the next time on her own and ever after.

Growing up on the fierce stream of the Elbe, emptying into the North Sea, there was that awesome respect, even fear of dykes breaking and flooding. I grew up, fascinated with the haunting tales of Theodor Storm. In particular "Der Schimmelreiter," where an island's dyke broke. When the ghost of a previous calamity appeared riding his white stallion along the breaking dyke, islanders knew they too would be called to the bottom of the sea. So legend said. Along the northern shores, starting with Denmark, then Germany and Holland, all of us experienced these water phenomena and learned to cope and live with the inevitable. First came the mighty storms, then flooding of river and sea, then dykes could break and did. Whole communities perished. The fertile *Alte Land*, north of us on the Elbe River, lay well below sea level like Holland, guarded by man's clever invention, dykes. Individual property lots were staked out with a trench or several trenches where water would drain the land, which had a visible high water table. Because of abundant water, grass was luscious green for animals to graze and fruit orchards produced in abundance, making it the fruit basket of western Germany. It was considered important for us to apprehend in our early school lessons the improved engineering feats of the dykes. With the ocean, Elbe and many lakes, it was high priority to learn to swim as young as possible. Yet the Elbe claimed many lives each summer. It was considered a great feat to swim across the river, dodging ferries, tugboats and ocean liners. Only the most experienced swimmers would dare. There was not much age difference between Ernst and myself so he wasn't awarded the title uncle. Ernst, who took a course in life saving, used me as a decoy, throwing me into the deep end of the *Fischteich*, then rescuing me after my considerable kicking about and panicking. Needless to say I made it high priority to learn to swim and he then lost interest in rescuing me. One summer Ernst rescued a woman who was caught in these fierce currents of the Elbe River. He safely returned her to the sandy beach. When a crowd gathered, he modestly walked away. I thought him a hero. Water, water everywhere.

Fridel had a passion for critters, mostly birds. A family friend researched birds, did magnificent photography and gave lectures during the winter months in his home. These weekly lectures must have been costly for us to afford, but miraculously my family supported this good endeavor for me to attend. Ardently I looked forward to each session on a wide variety of local birds. Yet with Fridel, birds of every kind became a passion for life and vastly enriched her life.

Hedi Hausen was a some time playmate as she was two years older, grossly overweight and tried to generate as little energy as possible. She lived at the end of my street in the biggest stucco house, painted all yellow. On their large property they raised pigs, chicken, geese and ducks, had fruit trees and a huge vegetable garden. While food was sparse, Hedi's family lived well and everyone was vastly overweight. On some rare occasion, I would be allowed to visit and play some table games in their kitchen. Hedi's energy depleted quickly and repeatedly she dashed into the pantry for nourishment. With her fore finger she dipped deeply into the crock of lard and devoured this big blob as if it was a most gourmet treat. Of course I was not asked if I too wanted a blob of that lard. I believe I would not have wanted to try it.

Occasionally Hedi came to our backyard property to fetch me for play on Höhnercamp. That day I had house arrest and talked to her out of the bedroom window. Repeatedly I'd warned her not to stand on the wooden platform over the sewer hole. Defiantly she ignored my warning, talking and gesturing, and suddenly she disappeared down the sewer hole. Regina, another sometime playmate just whisked away with the first racket of heart piercing screams. Frau Bohn, the landlady, customarily sat on the veranda afternoons enjoying coffee and cakes, but this day could not be seen. Surely these screams must have penetrated throughout every dwelling. No one came to help. Bare, only clad in panties, I jumped out of the window and started pulling and heaving Hedi's hand, which grasped the wooden ledge. Hedi was a big girl. She was the biggest girl in our entire school and I couldn't budge her. The stench of the sewer in which she was submerged closing in on her shoulders could have made her faint. Hedi wanted to live and she hung on for life. I am not sure how it all came about, but with our joint effort Hedi ended up standing in front of me, still screaming. Brown juice of sewer materials clung to her and ran off her, and more embarrassed than frightened now she ran home. It was the first time I had seen Hedi run. Later questions asked but never answered, why Regina ran away and Frau Bohn did not come to help? Why couldn't I have put on some clothing before jumping out of the window to help?'

A few at a time, the men came home from the front. Limbs were missing and they looked haggard. There was initial joy of couples and children reunited with fathers, but shortly after tension set in. Not by choice but for survival, women had become independent, managing their families and businesses as well as they could. Our immediate neighbors had managed a bakery, *Konditorei* - pastry shop, and a flourishing bar by three generations of women. The grandmother ran the bakery, the mother the bar and the daughter helped out where needed. Herbert the youngest stayed free of chores and was undisciplined. Men long absent, returned from the war with dreams and vigor to rebuild or create anew. Herr Körner, our neighbor, was a serious man with more ambitious dreams than most. Herbert his son was no longer seen idle. He was no longer seen at all. There were immense building projects in progress, improving the already stately enterprise. I wasn't sure if every family member embraced such totalitarian labor force. It was a time for readjustment and rebuilding a nation. The *Bauhaus* initially headed by Gropius in Weimar initiated the *Deutcher Werkbund* of artists - architects and craftsmen. New architecture emphasized clear, geometric shapes. Building designs were often clean, simple and rational - prefabricated what the *Bauhaus* labeled dwelling machines. The post-war population needed to be housed, and these were simple enough for the poor and therefore appropriate for all.

8 Growing up Despite Odds b

MY SISTER ELFRIEDE, Elfi nicknamed, was nearly absent from the memory of our growing up years. Four years younger than I, she received most of my mother's attention. I spent long periods away from home in camps. She was too young to join time spent with my friends. Furthermore, we alternated visiting my father in the *Harz* Mountains. Just like myself, Elfi too had to carve a path of her own. She had a demanding personality, and I didn't want to take orders from someone that much younger. She didn't make friends easily unless they were younger and compliant. She had better grades than I and was amply rewarded for those. When she wanted something, like ice cream or sweets, she only had to ask for it.

I would venture into the beloved woods, pick a two-liter can of blueberries, blackberries or red raspberries, baskets of mushrooms or whatever in season. When I returned from the woods or fields, there was joy with the goods I had brought home. I received a *Groschen,* about 10cents for my persistent labor. I deposited this treasure into my small metal savings box, which had a lock. Often I ventured into the woods to the delight of a hungry family. When I finally made the decision for a purchase from the many dimes I had saved, I found the box totally empty. The younger ones, Elfi and our young cousin living close, must have had a fine time spending my hard earned money.

Elfi excelled in sports just like our father had and I too. She started in a program training in running, high jumping. Her performances were record breaking and she was considered for training as an Olympic contestant. Raised with a free reign and little discipline, she started smoking at a young age. Sadly her performance level dropped.

I visited my father in the *Harz* with mixed feelings. He was reserved and very stern, and I could not feel close to him. He was my father, an isolated figure, perhaps too like my mother. He, *Tante* Gertrud, as I was to call my stepmother, and Norbert, my half-brother, lived in a remote village in cramped quarters by any standards, but life was peaceful in this rural enclave. Unemployed, my father pursued his research in optics with contact of like-minded associates.

During these visits he and I explored the beautiful woods and climbed steep hills and mountains at speeds that left me breathless. I trailed behind, as I was not accustomed to the high altitude coming from the flat lands at sea or below sea level. My father taught me to appreciate and respect nature. He taught me to pick edible mushrooms. I learned to identify plants and wild flowers. He was always searching to find out if I showed any scientific abilities.

So one early morning after breakfast, without much ado, I received a packed lunch, and we walked with record speed, as it was my father's custom, to Alfeld, the nearest town. I was instructed to remember the roads so I could return on my own in the afternoon. Then I was deposited at the *Technische Hochschule* for a morning of intensive testing.

I was appalled. At about age eleven to twelve my sexual identity had not yet been questioned or challenged. I was raised in a primarily female environment. We arrived late. Quietly I took an assigned seat for this in advance scheduled testing program. I found myself now in a formal all-boys academy of ages at least two or more years my seniors. In a casual setting the instructor

hovered over an automobile engine and everyone in lively manner contributed in the conversation. What was I doing here? I had
never seen an engine up close. Never did I expect to be confronted with one again either. Politely I passed the time with thoughts
of my own. The following math problems were far above my
comprehension and caring. We did drawings and puzzle solving
of a technical nature last, which did hold my interest and I was
able to complete the assignment well and rapidly.

Fortunately the results from the technical academy arrived
when I already had departed for Hamburg and the Kühlich clan.
My father must have been aghast. Since I showed neither interest nor participated in the engine discussion and proved inept at
the more complex math that I had no knowledge of, I received
the lowest rating of the group. Nevertheless I did show a strong
aptitude for art and the visual. From then on my father considered me retarded and introduced me as such to his associates.
No matter what I would attain in later years, my father did not
change his opinion despite that I would accomplish considerable
more than my siblings.

PART II
A New Beginning

9 Migrating to the USA

OUR STEPMOTHER TANTE Gertrud did not take to Elfi, my younger sibling by four years. She bitterly complained about this tender aged child in every way, unjustly I felt. In 1952, young and not accustomed to speak out, I wasn't able to defend her. There wasn't much more than a ten-year age difference between Tante Gertrud and me. She was a large woman, taller than my father, very strong physically, and boisterous. She was loud spoken except when being intellectually challenged by my father's associates. After minimum schooling she worked as a maid before marriage to my father. Remembering the cruel beatings my mother had received from my father when I was impressionable and very young, I was content that she was never to be physically mistreated by my father. Rather he had to mind himself and abide by her strong will.

I seemed to be the lesser of the undesirable children of her husband's previous marriage. Our relationship during those summer visits was civil. To make myself useful in this frugal household, I continued to spend time alone in the woods to pick wild berries of every kind in large containers. She aptly prepared juices and knew to preserve the bountiful harvest for the winter months. I received her appreciation for the quantities of diverse mushrooms I hauled out of the forest for many a tasty meal. Also I tried to make myself useful around the house but mostly entertained myself to free her to tend to her young son.

On one of our outings into the splendid mountainous woods of the Harz region, my father confronted me with the proposal that he, one of many scientists, was being considered for work in the United States of America. It meant he would be doing research in his own field, radiology, in which there wasn't a future for him after the war in Germany. Perhaps only a couple hundred physicists would be selected, but he was hopeful. Would I be interested in migrating with him to a new continent?

Ninth grade was coming to a close. What was in store for me? I showed aptitude in sewing. The only option open for me was to become a seamstress apprentice if indeed I was fortunate to be accepted into a clothing or tailoring workshop. Meanwhile a two-year security check on my father was coming to a close. He was one of two physicists chosen to contribute their knowledge in the United States. Elation of this news was brief. Now that security was in order, the company to hire my father demanded his departure immediately. Arrangements were made for the first available ship, in this case the SS *America*, March 1953, and the only space available was first class.

All happened with whirlwind speed. Herr Zülke, our teacher, had a hard time comprehending my departing for the land of freedom and opportunity with a father he was not even aware of. I had not participated in English, supposedly mandatory in this defeated land. I struggled with it briefly and decided that I wasn't made for it. One of the rare instances I recall that I outsmarted myself. Due to my father and family's early departure, I did not graduate with my class. Nor did I receive confirmation class rites in a group. Pfarrer - Pastor Hannes decided that I needed to be confirmed before setting out for America. With my closest friend, Gerlinde, I was confirmed in the Evangelische - Lutherische Kirche, in the only church and the only denomination in Rissen, in a solemn rite in the pastor's office. The family gathered to prepare a hurried confirmation celebration and farewell in our small apartment.

I needed still another medical examination for the immigration. Already I had every kind of vaccination, so I expected to be exempt from them. I had to journey into Hamburg, and with other immigrants in a large hall, we had the last check-up for our eligibility. As the youngest adult female, I was asked to stand separate from the group. A doctor knelt before me and without any privacy, with my legs spread, he examined my vagina, supposedly checking for venereal disease. I was at the tender age of fourteen and realized it had to be endured.

Everything my father owned was sold or disposed of. We were only able to take with us a very limited amount of weight, which my father mostly satisfied with books and papers. My weight allowances were a few pounds, which fit into a very small satchel to hold my earliest pencil and crayon drawings and some clothing.

The morning of my departure, my mother confronted me with a solemn speech to "trust in God." This surprised me, as I did not know her to be a religious person. We were not to see one another for many years, yet the parting was unemotional. Tante Ruth, my mother's younger sister, escorted me to Hamburg Hauptbahnhof, main train station, where I joined my father and his family. We had only a brief awkward introduction and then minimum time for few spoken words and unemotional good-byes. The train pulled out of the station to take us to the Elbe River harbor docks. We boarded the gigantic ocean liner *SS America*, at that time the second largest ocean liner after the *Queen Elizabeth*.

I learned that first, second and tourist classes were segregated. For the first time I saw black people, attendants, with the whitest teeth I had ever seen, who were most kind when I

**Tante Gertrud, myself, Norbert,
father Paul Weber, 1953**

needed help or had lost my bearings in this giant maze of endless hallways on numerous floors. Dining on American food was
a delight, at first, as my father, the only one to speak English,
translated the menu for us, not always correctly. Sometimes food
served turned out a surprise. I wore my new confirmation dress
and shoes and nylon stockings for dinner, but Tante Gertrud put
a stop to this, and I had to wear my old outfit, consisting of an ill
fitting skirt and blouse. This was the only other outfit I owned. As
a young child I used to watch the ocean liners from the beaches,
escorted by smaller boats guiding them to the open sea, then
we'd jump into the water to catch those giant salty tasting waves,
generated by powerful propellers. Now we clutched the railing
on this cold windy day of March 1953 for a last glimpse of what

was home. To the north were the tall dykes hiding the fruit farms of das *Alte Land* and stately homes well below sea level. This was considered the fruit basket for West Germany.

We passed Ireland, the perfectly luscious green gem in the Atlantic Ocean, with what seemed the last rays of sun. A storm was brewing in the open sea. It was standard safety procedure for each passenger to put on life jackets and hover close to our assigned emergency boats. Initial joy of these hovering waves, a house or two tall, soon made my stomach twist with agony. It was called seasickness, and I had made up my mind not to be afflicted by this silly ailment. From that day on I stayed in my bunk, not able to take any food or liquid. The only time I left the cabin was when I had profuse frightening nosebleeds, taking my breath away and requiring me to see the ship doctor. I had decided adamently not to get seasick, yet it was a joke, because I was one of the first to succumb to this malady and the very last to recover. I had to miss out on on all the fun activities like movies, games, use of swimming pool and dining. Nearly everyone became seasick for some time. Norbert at age almost four did not complain of any discomforts.

Close to ten days of this coasting the frantic waves had to be endured, then news broke, "land in sight." My father made the firm announcement that he wasn't going to carry me off the boat, and I had better get to the deck as we were approaching the magnificent New York skyline we were familiar with from photographs. I felt feeble and passive, having stayed in the cabin for so many days, though the fresh breeze on the open deck felt invigorating. We saw the landmark for freedom as we passed the East River on Manhattan Island, the Statue of Liberty. For many, a hard life's journey had come to offer new hopes. Some passengers wept. All of us were emotionally affected by this awesome sight, of the sculpture of lady liberty, a gift of the French government, hailing freedom and welcoming us to the American shore.

My father's security clearance was intact so our stay on Ellis Island was brief. Onkel Reinhold exuberantly welcomed us on dock. He was my grandmother's younger brother, the first and only other family immigrant. An aeronautical engineer, he worked his entire life at Bruster Corporation, which had lost out on government war contracts to Boeing, until his retirement in 1957. His wife followed him to America, just before the outset of WWI. His departure was due to not agreeing with German politics of the time. At his death at 95, in 1990, a ten-year age discrepency was discovered, so a new birth certificate was issued, aging him 105 at his death. Our European family had long suspected some espionage activities might be the reason for altering his age and name. By correspondence he had stayed close to his family in Germany. As my grandmother's first grandchild, I received a warm welcome, and he even detected a family resemblance to his dear sister. He took us home to Bellaire on Long Island, where we spent a day to rest and to be initiated in the American ways. After all, we were greenhorns, what all new immigrants were called, and we had much to learn.

10 Fitting into a New Family

OUR IMMIGRATION DOCUMENTS and my father's security clearance were intact and our stay on Ellis Island was brief. *Onkel* Reinhold exuberantly welcomed us on dock. He was my grandmother's younger brother, the first and only other family immigrant. As young lutendant, he had disagreed with the Kaiser's politics and arrived in America just prior to WW I. He worked as an aeronautical electrical engineer for R.R.B. until his retirement. Early in his career, his work took him to California and on extensive travels throughout South America. In the new country, he changed his name to Winterfield, and we honestly believe he was an agent. His young bride Alma Kröger joined him in 1916 voyaging on the *Lusetania*. On the very next ocean passing, this vessel was torpedoed by a German submarine. This incident consequently provoked the United States to enter WWI in 1917. Their only daughter, Hellen, was born in 1918. In correspondence and spirit, he had stayed close to his family in Germany. Receiving his care packages after the end of World War II was our first introduction to American delicacies of packaged food like chocolate powder, Jell-O pudding and clothing, all of which seemed such an extravagance. Those packages brought great joy and amusement, as the clothes were not easily wearable. Both he and his wife, *Tante* Alma were to stay my closest and dearest relations in the United States during their life time. As *Onkel* Reinhold's older sister's first grandchild, I received a warm welcome, and he even detected a family resemblance to his dear sister. He took us home to his wife in Bellaire on Long Island where they lived in an immaculate, flower imbedded, large home at a corner intersection. We rested up for a day in their protective company and listened to advice of what to be aware of. After all we were greenhorns, what all newly arrived immigrants are called and treated as such. The coming morning we proceeded by train to upstate New York, destination Buffalo, where my father's employment was awaiting him.

The first immigrants of our family arriving before WW1. Myself with Tante Alma and Onkel Reinhold Winterfield.

Could I have still been affected by seasickness? Memory of that train ride remains a blur. Weak and despondent, having taken little food for the past ten days and very ill at sea, I now took a window seat letting the wide open spaces and towns glide by. My father angrily turned on me, as he expected me bright and alert focussing on the new country.

My father's employer had arranged a furnished apartment in a two-story building, which we occupied on the lower level. The middle-aged landlord had just been widowed, and I was to occupy the room and bed his wife had just died in. All the houses on either side of the wide street, lined with very tall old shady elm trees, were painted gray, identical with their tall porches and patches of grass in the front yard. One had to remember the house number or else walk on without ever finding the right house. We couldn't help compare this to what we'd left behind. I'd never seen row houses. Every house in Rissen or other German towns I'd seen had its distinct architecture and uniqueness. Buffalo was an industrial town, often with dark smokey skies. Was this America? Was this the country I had romantically fantasized? Winter snows were beyond our wildest imagination with below freezing temperatures we were not accustomed to. Schools, even businesses, had to be closed for days as we valiantly shoveled ourselves out from under this white deluge. My father was informed that men often suffered heart attacks coping with such abundance of snow. So then it became my sole responsibility to shovel a path on the sidewalk in front of our house and on the one leading to the side entrance, tunneling myself through snows up to my shoulder. Although there was another family renting above us, snow shoveling and the entire summer yard work of mowing and weeding rested with me.

With our limited command of English, grocery shopping

82

was fun and a challenge, trying to figure out what to buy. But we missed the food we had been accustomed to. We coped with a new language and new traditions. By contract my father was to work towards his doctorate, and he immediately complied by signing up for classes at the university. Not long after, he claimed that he knew more than his professors did, and working towards that degree seemed to him an endless waste of time. He quit. The other stipulations on the contract he had to keep. His work of research was not to be disclosed to anyone, not even family, and he could never return to his homeland, Germany. I was to return to my mother after a two-year stay with a rather remote father and hostile stepmother, but that subject was not approached again. We all were homesick, but nothing could be done about that. Norbert, age four, seemed to enjoy everything new, most of all ice cream, television, and frosted birthday cakes, and he adopted quickest to the new language.

I was to continue grammar school until mid June 1953 before attending high school in September. *Tante* Gertrud had taken firm control of the household chores, and her iron will prevailed. The first day when I returned home from all day in classes, in the late afternoon, I met *Tante* Gertrud at the threshold of the kitchen. She had just washed the kitchen floor. By now I was duly intimidated by her harsh manners towards me. Annoyed, she asked me to step inside. I waited in the door entrance, hesitant about stepping on the still wet floor. Accompanied by her screeching voice, she tossed the dripping floor rag clear across my face from the far side of the kitchen. What brought this on? She only had a grammar school education, and she was already working, hired out as a maid, cleaning houses at my age. Now I was continuing school, four more years mandatory in this new world. She could not have anticipated this when planning to come to the US. My father was education minded, and I knew he supported my schooling to the point that I wasn't even allowed part-time work until I mastered the language. I never tried as hard before or after to please and appease anyone with as little success. Why was I asked to join their family? I suspected my father did not want to pay child support for my sister and myself, this was an appeasement to my mother, when leaving Germany for him to furnish my sole support. *Tante* Gertrud had dreams of a better lifestyle and owning her own home. She had started work at my age and now was hoping for an extra income and someone to do the housework, someone to be her maid. At my father's suggestion, *Tante* Gertrud and I signed up for an evening course to speed up learning the language. She only attended the first session. She did not feel like venturing out evenings. I completed the course, and thereafter looked for every kind of opportunity to be absent from the house.

Neighbors with a daughter a couple of years younger started inviting me to their country home for weekends. It was a lovely but brief respite from the harsh treatments at home. *Tante* Gertrud soon became annoyed with my weekend departures. She insisted that her son Norbert should be invited as well. At age four the kind neighbors felt it would require too much care taking and so the invitations stopped, cooling the relationship.

We met only a few recent immigrants in the area. Sophie Battha was Hungarian with already a good command of English and of German as well, so in school she was assigned to translate for me. She was a tall attractive brunette, and we became good friends. Sophie hoped to aspire to become a librarian and was an avid reader. Her father had been one of the leading heads of the Hungarian government, and the family had been well to do. At the end of war, as the communist regime took over, families of leading government officials were disposed of, sometimes assassinated, if they weren't fortunate enough to escape. The couple with their five children and one loyal servant took refuge in Germany. Here too the family was persued by communists as well. Their lives threatened they eventually found means in the humblest way in transit on open deck of a small ocean liner to migrate to the new world, and ended up in Buffalo. The children had been raised by governesses and spoke several languages fluently. Sophie kindly assisted me in English, and I helped her with math, which she didn't much care for. Her family now sustained themselves working at menial jobs, living on memories of more glorious days. We each longed to be elsewhere.

My father had made the acquaintance of a family from work. They came Sundays for coffee, cake and pastries, *Tante* Gertrud was a master of baking for which she was amply praised. The couple was educated in Tel Aviv. The husband was a physicist, and the wife was a mathematician. I greatly admired the woman as I had never before come in contact with a woman who capably worked in a man's world in such a meaningful position. A light dawned, a woman can... At times I was volunteered to baby sit for their two lovely young daughters. One afternoon as our families gathered, the physicist inquired of me what I hoped to aspire to. Without hesitation I responded that I hoped to become a fashion designer and an artist. My father paled and with the corners of his thin lip turned down, he replied, "she is retarded, she will never aspire to anything." Deadly silence followed.

11 Rochester on Lake Ontario

DURING MY FRESHMAN year in 1953 – 4, I attended consecutively three high schools as we made our transition from Buffalo to Rochester on Lake Ontario. Coping with a new language was a challenge at best. Under these circumstances my grades were poor, and my father felt justified to consider and treat me as retarded. These were my most sensitive teenage years. I had no anchor. There wasn't a confidante to share my troubled home life with. I lived with a dictionary and made a valiant effort to absorb, to fit into a new family and into the American way.

I attended the first high school only for several months that school year. The only other immigrant was another multi-lingual classmate, a Polish girl, who was asked to assist me. The furor erupted in science class. Math and science were easy, as they did not require as much English as other subjects. My test grades were high, identical to the classmates seated around me. Infuriated, with strong reprimands for cheating, the teacher sent me to the principal. This was the first and only time I had to report to a principal for a reprimand. Frightened I entered the principal's office. Aware of my family records, the principal was informed of my father being a physicist, and he believed in my honesty during testing. In subsequent tests I was isolated from the other students, and I still continued to receive high grades. The other students, who had previously surrounded me, including the Polish girl, did not do as well.

My father attended his first parent conference, and I was very apprehensive. He seemed to have been gone a long time.

Incomprehensible to him, all teachers had something good to report about me. Yes, understandably I struggled, there was the language difficulty, but I tried really hard. My father was most eager to meet with my science teacher. Upon identifying himself, he volunteered that he was a research physicist, and he was interested in talking about science. The teacher paled, and he stuttered, "then you know so much more than I do," and with that, he abruptly turned and left my father to himself. It was the only parent conference my father attended during my high school years. Soon after we moved, and I attended another school.

Leaving Buffalo had been easy. Sophie in her own unhappy way envied me. As it turned out, all were much happier in Rochester. There were lovely parks, sandy beaches, clear skies, and my father seemed to prefer his new assignment. We now moved to a primarily Polish and Lithuanian neighborhood and adapted well into this immigrant area. The house in which we rented the second floor, two-bedroom apartment belonged to an elderly immigrant Lithuanian couple with their last remaining daughter still living at home. Maja, about ten years older than myself, was tall, large boned, with delicate fair skin, lovely white blond hair, and very pale blue eyes. She seemed very attractive to me and so much more mature than myself. Her parents were very kind to me in a secretive way, which I then could not understand. They must have been aware, by my stepmother's screaming tantrums and her critical ways with me, that I was an unwanted child.

One day the couple appeared at our back door, and made an offer for me as a teenager to use the single attic room to be more private, at no extra cost. Most touchingly, the elderly husband had freshly painted the whole room, with slanting walls and ceiling, in the happiest brightest pink. Deep in my heart I gave thanks to the Lord. Of course *Tante* Gertrud found fault with the color and the room. Norbert now had the bedroom to himself on their level, but it was decided that I would share my room with his electric train, rails covering the whole floor making it hard to dust. The noisy commotion intruded on my privacy as well. Furthermore my father installed a large gray metal cabinet to house his extensive files and books. Between both of them using the room, I was left with little privacy. I was allowed little time in the room and had to study in the small dining room with constant intrusion and criticism. I had to turn in early at night with lights out and was checked up not to be reading. Not yet tired, I overheard their conversations clearly through the floor heating vent. No matter how hard I tried to appease *Tante* Gertrud, and I was in great fear of her verbal outbursts, she found a barrage of my transgressions to report to my father. This she intermingled with my sister's shortcomings, who had only briefly stayed with them years ago. Once I overheard my father speak up in my defense just to be overruled. I closed the shutters of the heating vent and covered it with a cloth for good. I felt so helpless, so vulnerable. What to do? I lacked the maturity and confidence to fend for myself if I ran away. Penniless, where could I run to? I was without US citizenship papers and that would complicate matters. Marriage was not an option, although some older working fellow immigrants had shown interest in me. I remembered my mother's vulnerable stage that led to marriage.

Years later I met Maja with her husband, her kindly parents had long passed away. The husband, a fellow Lithuanian and some years older, was not patient, and complained about his wife being very spoiled. Maja's beautiful pale blue eyes searched mine, pointing her index finger into my face, exclaiming with a strong accent, that I was the sole source of it. "Barbara's fault." She confronted me with the fact that her parents had been aware of my mistreatment and helplessness, therefore showered their own daughter with great love and more latitude.

Benjamin Franklin High School was the third school I attended that year but from here I also graduated. So I couldn't run away and with no immediate plan for my future, I just concentrated on finishing high school, doing the best I knew. Only one of us few foreigners, one particular German friend, Waltraut, went on to college, being tutored to pass the entrance exams.

Math again was the easiest subject. My father's opinion of me fluctuated, either voicing his opinion that I was retarded or that he hoped I'd turn out to be another Madame Curie collaborating as his assistant. If I would study physics, he'd send me to college. I did not want to uphold his dreams and gave math and science minimum attention but dropped the courses as soon as I could. Emil Maurer, the art teacher, and I had a warm relationship. He immediately recognized my ability, and I could do no wrong. He allowed me, a lowly freshman, to work on a senior project, the yearbook. Chess was the overall theme, and I was allowed to illustrate the inside front and back cover. I chose check mat. Never having played chess, I implored my father, a chess champion among his brilliant friends to show me a check mate move. He offered to play a game of chess with me to the chess mate position. My only interest was in the deciding position so I could make a sketch of it. He explained the moves to me, and we played for some time. Dinner was being served so he wanted to finish the game quickly. The moves he suggested did not seem advantageous to me. I plotted my own course. He became angry when I prolonged the game. Finally we arrived at check mate. His face paled and grew angrier now. I had won. Miraculously his friends couldn't beat him, and here a female, his daughter, had won. It was a hard lesson learned. He didn't talk to me for three days.

We were only a few German immigrants in high school. We stayed close and only spoke our native language among ourselves for which the teachers reprimanded us. Assimilation therefore took longer and I retained an accent. On occasions I was invited to someone's church, eager for any reason to escape home. I was never allowed to return a second time. One pastor came to visit our house to ask permission for me to attend his services and partake in the youth program. I was impressed how well versed my father was with the scriptures, claiming to be agnostic, and how eloquently he fended off the pastor. *Tante* Gertrud explained that Sunday was a day for me catch up on housework, my only free time. My chores were cleaning the bathroom, polishing the families shoes worn during the entire week, doing so on the floor of the back porch, cleaning the front and back stairs leading to the apartment, ironing my father's white shirts, family mending, peeling potatoes, vegetables and washing dishes at all times. During one Sunday dinner the usual ordering me around came. Now five year old Norbert, with whom I had a warm relationship, emphatically chirped up, "you treat Barbara just like Cinderella, Barbara do this, Barbara do that, all day long." *Tante* Gertrud had a very hard time quieting him down.

As every teenage girl must mature into womanhood, she becomes more feminine and lovely. Considered the ugly duckling in my family on the other side of the Atlantic, I too now blossomed. Friends and acquaintances of the family complimented my looks and charm. Not accustomed to compliments of any kind, I was not only embarrassed but fear struck deep into my heart that *Tante* Gertrud would retaliate in word and deed, as she was never complimented for her appearance. German families gathered for all kinds of social functions, dinners, dances and concerts. It was suggested to my father that I should partake as contestant for Miss Germany - America of our region. For once I was grateful for his strong denial as I was very shy.

Onkel Reinhold kept a prolific correspondence with all of the relatives and now graciously included us, especially us, as we were so few on this hemisphere. For my summer school break he and *Tante* Alma invited me to their home in Bellaire, Long Island. My father responded that he could not afford to send me, but *Onkel* Reinhold sent a roundtrip Greyhound bus ticket. In my father's household, I was intimidated and was afraid of every move, every word spoken, every gesture as it surely would be met with harsh reprisal. At *Onkel* Reinhold's house, never had I lived in a peaceful, accepting and warm environment such as I was to partake with my dear relatives for these two summer vacations. *Onkel* Reinhold was close to retiring but he was strong and energetic. Perhaps his best feature was his indefatigable good humor. Clearly immigrants, after having spent most of their lives in America, they talked much about the old country and their overseas relatives. A good natured quarrel came about. Their only daughter, *Tante* Lenchen insisted, that I should spend time with her family the Eckhoffs in Pennsylvania. So *Onkel* Reinhold and *Tante* Alma went for a brief visit to my father's family in Rochester.

Staying with the Eckhoffs turned into a joyous visit. The boys, Martin and Thomas, were precious as we played, went swimming, and I read to them stories or we conversed in German. *Onkel* Martin, who came from the Hamburg suburbs, "das Alte Land," was physically handicapped, but I discovered could do more than an able bodied man. Accustomed to be kept busy with chores, I was engulfed in a loving family with many relaxing times. *Tante*

Lenchen wanted to keep me for the summer, but then it was amiably worked out that I would divide time between them as *Onkel* Reinhold was very personable and loved company.

Over one of our leisurely lunches, *Tante* Alma approached the subject of my coming to live with them, and they had even discussed adopting me. Apparently their visit to the Weber's had not gone well. *Tante* Alma confided that in my father's profession he needed a more refined wife. *Tante* Gertrud must have acted herself, loud, outspoken, using bad or vulgar language. Only when intellectually challenged by my father's associates did she keep quiet. Even then, with my dear relatives I was afraid to speak up, but my ill treatment seemed apparent. At the tender age of fifteen, I realized it had to be endured. Yet fear of retaliation, not being a citizen and my own feeling of inability kept me tied to my father.

At the end of the summer my relatives reluctantly parted with me. When an invitation came forth again for following summer vacations, it was decided that I could go only on condition of taking Norbert go with me. There was too much of an age difference, too much looking after a rambunctious young boy for an elderly couple. It turned out that I got a job working part time until the end of my high school summers, and I was no longer free to visit with my dearest relatives.

12 Promise of a Career

WITHOUT MUCH AIM one day passed another. My father worried that he may have to support me for the rest of his days and prompted me to take a typing course. Since I didn't show any marketable skills, he hoped that I would be fit for office work. Typing proved to be a valuable asset, but even in that course I did poorly. I needed practice to bring up my typing speed. My father's antique German typewriter, on which he tipped away with two fingers, had an excess of characters not in the English language, and therefore the layout differed. At this time my father noticed a want ad for a fashion illustrator at B. Forman Co. advertising studio. B. Forman Co. was a retail store where we didn't shop. It was the most exclusive shop in Rochester, therefore the least affordable for us. My father suggested I stop by at the studio, show some of my sketches and inquire what preparation and education that job required. So I set out as directed. The art director, John Lancatella, was tall, dark, handsome and willing to look at my fashion drawings. Apparently he was not impressed since he didn't make a statement about them. He pulled out some illustrations he himself had done of children and fashion merchandise, shoes and gloves. He handed me two sheets of illustration board and inks used by commercial studios for newspaper reproduction, some brushes and a sketching pen. I was to copy the works and return for his review.

This was at the end of my sophomore year. At home I was allowed to work on the round dining room table, white lace tablecloth removed. The small dining room was a thoroughfare to other rooms, a busy place full of commotion. Norbert was close at hand and showed a keen interest in what I was doing. Dieter had just been born, wailing in his crib at my side, and *Tante* Gertrude was ever fiercely bustling and cleaning. Excitedly I set to work, copying exactly what was before me, following every minute detail. For the first time I applied washes, without instructions, just following instincts as it required knowledge I didn't yet have.

John Lancatella was perplexed. The drawings were identical to every detail. However I had been given a less expensive paper to draw on, and that was the only way he could tell the works apart. Excitedly he called in the senior illustrator and other personnel. I showed talent but did not have an education and training. The field was very specialized, so a number of graduates from Rochester Institute of Technology came for a week, a few hours each evening, to illustrate various items of clothing, furs, shoes and handbags, jewelry. Then selection would be made for one artist trainee. I was invited as well to participate in this competition. Humbly I selected the drawing table in the far corner near the studio window. I considered it a great privilege to be invited to participate in this group of college graduates, and I would just chalk up the exposure as experience. Perhaps later, much later, I thought to enter this profession with some schooling.

We numbered about half a dozen, occupying small drawing desks that Monday evening after working hours. Eagerly we followed instructions to sketch a daytime dress, which was attractively draped on a store mannequin. We worked a couple of hours each night, and I so thoroughly enjoyed this experience that I didn't pay attention to the other graduates, as it was beyond my comprehension or ambition to compete. Tuesday evening we were asked to sketch an elegant full length mink coat, again

3

draped on a mannequin. We were one less graduate already as she had decided this work was not for her. I found sketching a fur the greatest challenge but I concentrated on the privilege of partaking. Just to do the very best seemed to become my motto without too much worrying about the result. I enjoyed the challenge, and we all struggled with this assignment. Wednesday we elaborated techniques in shoes and handbags of leather, patent leather, suede and reptile. Where was everyone? Only Bob and I showed up. Timid and naïve, he had to confront me with the fact it was too much of a challenge for most. He only continued to participate for the experience. He announced, Barbara you're it. Someone must have been watching over me. Someone must have been looking out for me for a long time. This was a great change in my life. This was the beginning of a new life - the beginning of a career.

With much fanfare, because of my age and inexperience, I was hired part-time to work as illustrator trainee after school, and on Saturdays, and then full-time during summer school break. John Lancatella called me a prodigy, a word I had to look up in the dictionary. I loved the work and the atmosphere of studio life. This incredible break made life worth living. I did have a hard time coping with the attention and acclamation I continued to receive. Store buyers and department heads came to our studio to observe me drawing. Some insisted that only I should illustrate their merchandise. Not accustomed to kind words or to flattery, I was embarrassed and was at a loss for words and blushed frequently I'm sure.

At high school, now entering my junior year, it too became known that almost daily some of my illustrations appeared in the Rochester newspapers. Benjamin Franklin High School had a few thousand students, less than a handful of immigrants, all

German, yet everyone seemed to know me. Here too I wished to hide from the admiring glances and gestures as I passed in the hallways to my classes. This came with the job, being called a prodigy, and I had to live with the recognition. My friends chided me for being so shy but this recognition I could do without, and in the future would never be able to embrace. I was to get some awards for drawings in the yearbook during school assembly. I never missed school for being sick, rarely did I catch a cold, but for these assemblies I shied the limelight and found an excuse to stay home.

Over breakfast, as my father glanced through the morning paper, I had to point out which of the drawings were mine. He never cared for any of them, they were too stylized, not realistic enough for his taste. He did not consider it art. Nor was a single drawing of mine ever displayed in their home.

13 A Dream is Born

I RECEIVED MINIMUM wages at B. Forman studio, but to me it was a fortune earned for a labor of love. From my first paycheck, I paid for a visit to a dentist. I just wanted a check up as I did not have any pain or a problem. Only once before had I visited a dentist in Germany. *Tante* Gertrud and Norbert attended the same friendly dentist next and both required major dental work due to long neglect. My father never went to see a dentist or doctor, because he always felt well. A medical checkup also proved me healthy, very slender and not very strong but OK. My needs were modest. Not being accustomed to spending money, I started to put my income into savings until I had a plan.

Illustrating at B. Forman advertising studio was still a welcome challenge but I could not see myself pursuing this career for the rest of my life. My spirits ran high. Take a risk, I told myself. My dream was still to become a fashion designer, to create fashions, not just sketch what others created. To realize this goal I needed an education, and I would save up every nickel and dime to realize this dream. Yes, a dream was born. I would save up tuition to attend a fashion design school in New York City. I now had a goal, and I could now tolerate anything. Life was exciting. I offered to pay for my keep but my father was education minded and allowed me to continue to save towards my goal.

John Lancatella became more critical of my fashion drawings. He said I lacked knowledge of the figure beneath the garment. The studio sent me to attend life drawing classes at Rochester Institute of Technology for evening sessions. College art classes opened another realm. I still was naïve and immature as I faced a nude model for the first time. Female models were totally in the bare but men at that time still wore a G - string. That first night I still fought the newness. Quick warm up poses of one - three - five and ten minutes followed the more relaxing twenty-minute poses. My intimidation gave way to my desire to master the most challenging exercise of drawing the human figure. We had an exceptional model who not only looked different but who was willing to take more difficult and challenging poses. Coco claimed to be an Arabian Gypsy, and no one doubted him. Each of the students claimed to have gotten their best drawings from his poses. He was well built and had a most exotic appearance.

Also I took advanced sewing and tailoring courses to prepare me for my journey ahead. John Lancatella asked to have a talk with my father at the studio. Of course I was apprehensive about this meeting, as I was aware how negative my father felt about my becoming an artist. When I later asked him about the meeting, he replied with the minimum of words, art is a breadless profession. John Lancatella insisted that although I was very talented, I still needed an education.

By now I had built up a small portfolio of some of my published fashion drawings and started to take the next step of interviewing with an advertising agency. I was still in high school but with an already published body of work. This further inspired awe and opened doors to the professional world. One art director told me a college graduate had just been hired, who didn't seem as competent or gifted as I was. I had to endure more admiration and being called a prodigy. Rumrill & Co. Advertising Agency provided me with my first freelance assignments to be published in national magazines. It was important to me to finish high school in order to keep a possibility open someday to attend college. At B. Forman studio I obtained training to further my career, and so at night, in my little pink attic room, I did my first freelance assignments, balancing a wooden drawing board on my lap. Life was worth living. I was preparing for independence and a move to one of the biggest and toughest world renown art and fashion centers.

Occasionally, as junior artist, I was asked to hand deliver some promotional works to the television studio. At my first visit, the director took me aside to discuss my being screen tested by Eastman Kodak for some television commercials. Already on some occasions I modeled for a still photographer at our studio for which I was paid extra. Obviously, not being of legal age and I always looked even younger, I needed my father's written consent. Modeling paid many times minimum wage, and it would have better prepared me for my schooling. My father was furious at this request. As on some other occasions, my father threatened, "you will find your suitcases packed and waiting for you on the front porch."

14 Recollections of New York City a

WAS IT ALL a dream?

Is this a dream?

I felt exuberant. New York City, May 1958. I celebrated my nineteenth birthday shortly after arriving in the city. I had been raised overly sheltered in my father's household since coming to the US just five years earlier. Nothing could have prepared me for stepping out alone into this metropolis. Up to this point all decisions had been made for me. I was to think what the elders thought best of. Even my clothes were selected for me, and I hoped to aspire to become a fashion designer. The women in my family and those of friends were secretaries until married and then became housewives. Period. It was audacious for me to have a career, and the very least, a career that would take me to the biggest cities. I yearned for an education, an education beyond the mandatory high school. College was not necessarily affordable for those early immigrants. I had not even heard of scholarships or grants. Although not taught or encouraged to think for myself, I had a dream of what I wanted of my life. I was not even aware that I was an independent or rebellious thinker, not a follower, so important to the artist I was to become.

I did not depart with the blessings of my family. When my bags were packed for the journey from Rochester to New York, my stepmother, I was to call her *Tante* Gertrud, motioned me aside for our last talk. Since I really was to depart, and did not plan to return, fear of her fierce words and manners no longer affected me as strongly. She reclined on the living room couch as usual, a large woman not used to exercise, while I was to stand before her for this last lecture. For all these years I lived with them, there was nothing she really could affront me with. As the child of my father's former marriage, she confessed, "I was therefore a constant reminder of her husband's former wife, your mother." That final revelation exposed to me that she didn't have the grace to overcome her jealousy and insecurity.

My total belongings consisted of two small suitcases, one of clothing and one filled with my earliest drawings and some art supplies, and two round hat boxes. With those, my father and I departed for the railroad station by bus. I was going to take the train to New York City. Due to my father being most conscientious, for whatever occasion, we always arrived early. He was a good talker and giving speeches was his forte. I was prepared. "Bärbel, you are not going to make it. You are destined for failure.

Touring Manhattan Island, free at last, 1958

Although you desire to meet failure, you are allowed to return to us. Art is a breadless profession." The attributes of working as secretary were then again reiterated. I tucked away this information for future reference. Furthermore, he said, "do not ever sign your name to any document before reading the fine print," and as I knew him not to be a religious person, "always walk a straight path." The train pulled in and noisily came to a stop. My father then helped to accommodate my luggage in the compartment and with a handshake departed before the train left.

Sitting back passively, from my window seat I took in New York state's scenery of mellow pastures, the five finger lakes, small and larger towns. What to do next? A year ago with a group of Japanese friends I had taken my only other trip to New York City. With Mary Lou I had stayed in the Tatham House YWCA a couple of nights while we explored the city. That would be my next destination. Comforted with that thought, I relaxed.

My alarm rang early the following morning, I was eager to start my new life. Washing up thoroughly in the tiny sink of the small Y room, I meticulously dressed. I owned two summer skirts and two winter skirts, some blouses to match, all I had sewn myself. I packed one of the identical hatboxes with what I anticipated for my first day's needs. Before departing for the day, I paid up ahead for another night at the Y. Then I walked to save the 15 cents subway token from 38th street to uptown Broadway at 52nd street.

At 1680 Broadway I took the elevator to the top floor. It was the pent house studio of Traphagen School of Fashions. I first stepped out to the garden, overlooking New York skyline from the 15th floor. Since my first part-time job I had saved every dime to fulfill my dream of becoming a fashion designer and an artist. My first choice had been FIT, Fashion Institute of Technology. It was a four-year program and I didn't have enough saved even for one year tuition. Traphagen offered a three-year program, and I was able to pay the first year tuition with a little money left over until I found part-time work to support myself. It was no small matter being here today. I had been informed by the school that I wasn't of age and that I needed my parents' consent to attend the school and they were as well to mail in the tuition. In good faith I had transferred the money into my father's account so he could make the tuition payment. The money just sat in his account and the deadline was quickly approaching for payment, or I was notified, that I needed to wait for the coming year to be accepted. I was deeply troubled. What to do if I couldn't go to NYC? I felt so vulnerable, so dependent. *Tante* Gertrud surmised that the money belonged to them. After all they had paid for my boat fare to the USA, paid for my support. During high school I worked part-time. After graduation I had a full-time job at a small salary, but immediately I offered to pay for my keep. My father being education minded, then thought it was a good idea to get some more schooling, even if it was as useless as art. So I was allowed to save up the tuition. It was a struggling matter for them to justify keeping the money. Finally my father did decide to mail the tuition payment just before the deadline for student admission expired.

Traphagen was to be home for me for the next two semesters. My courses included draping and design, pattern making, grading, dressmaking, finishing a sample book, sketch class, fashion design and I loved it all. Our main teacher, like a mother hen, took us all under her caring wing.

That first late afternoon after classes, I checked out the *New York Times* section for apartment rentals. The first search for an apartment took me well up the east side by subway. Eventually the doorbell was answered by a kindly mannered heavy set man of the deepest black skin color. It was a basement apartment that was advertised for rent and he didn't want to show it to me. "You don't belong here," he answered. "Do you know where you are? This is Harlem." I did not know what Harlem meant, but he asked me to find another apartment elsewhere.

So the next evening I checked out another apartment just a few blocks from school, right off Broadway in a very old building with a dark staircase. A small deformed older woman answered the door and showed me a windowless, sparsely furnished room that was for rent in their apartment. I thought this would get me out of the Y and eventually I would find something more accommodating. She explained that she and her husband had been working the trapeze in the circus when she fell and was injured. Hard times had befallen them. I paid for the week and moved in the next day. It was an inhospitable room, so I didn't even unpack my suitcases. Each day had been filled with many events, at night I was exceedingly tired and slept well. During the first night a strong male voice approached my door, demanding to see that German girl. Yes, I had a distinct accent. The husband, whom I had met only briefly, sounded intoxicated. I figured due to having left an exciting circus career, he had escaped reality with alcohol. As the pounding on my door became more demanding, I quickly barricaded the door with whatever furnishings there were available plus I used my two suitcases and the two hatboxes for additional support. Truly intimidated I stayed awake that night as the calling and pounding on my door continued for most of the night it seemed. I had not been given the opportunity to assert myself in my short life, but the very next morning I confided in the compassionate teacher, and Mrs. Pizzo agreed that I had to move.

14 Recollections of New York City b

A FRIEND FROM Rochester had given me a contact, a woman he knew who might be looking for a roommate. I wanted to handle this 'getting started' on my own, plus I was exceedingly shy. So most hesitantly I made the call to introduce myself. Judith Doty already knew about me. Promptly she asked to meet me at her upper West Side brownstone apartment for us to get acquainted. So for the third day after classes I set out to explore the housing situation.

Judith was 5'4" tall, two inches shorter than I was. She was very attractive and in her mid twenties as I already knew. Beautiful long brown hair with tight curls around her head framed her even featured face. Slender, with the figure of a dancer, her intense, intelligent gaze sized me up instantly. I felt at that moment that she had totally assessed me, which proved to be correct. Overwhelmed I took in the luxurious décor of her apartment. She came from Washington state and her family was well to do. Graciously she offered me a seat and a glass of wine. Comforted, she now presented her plan. She assured me that I had arrived just at precisely the right moment. Judith was an actress. Upon arriving in New York City, she immediately was accepted for a Broadway play, *The Diary of Anne Frank*, in which she played the sister of Anne Frank. She was an instant success. She relished in that part of stardom until the play closed. She was auditioning for other roles while her parents temporarily supported her. But now this had come to an end. She had come on hard times. With much verbal flare, the gifted actress eloquently related her situation. Already she had located another, smaller apartment off Riverside Drive, not far from this present apartment. She needed a roommate. Was I willing to look at the apartment, which was in walking distance?

So we came to share an apartment on 82nd Street, a couple of blocks west of Broadway, and then another block farther from us was Riverside Park on the Hudson River. It was one of those typical New York brownstone houses. We occupied the fifth floor which was also the top. Ours had a tower, which extended our living room. The windows faced Broadway, straight across 82nd street, and we had a view of the park as well. It was a narrow five-floor walk-up building. No need to exercise. Even in prime youth, it could be debated whether a round trip down and up the dark staircase was absolutely necessary. To check the mailbox had to be incorporated with another outing. The living room was spacious and bright due to the tower windows. There was a very small kitchen nook, which we hardly ever used. The bathroom had a large skylight and there was only one small bedroom. This was something we could afford jointly. Judith was in control. I had never had a rommate and I was an eager student. We shared the only closet, but we each had our own dresser, and I was to take the bedroom. As she explained, she stayed up late and would be entertaining at times, so it would be best if she took the living room sofa. We each seemed to be content with that.

Judith was worldly and I had much to learn. When I arrived from school those first few evenings, we talked and got to know each other. Then Judith packed some bags and left to stay with Michael. Michael Colligrassi was the steady boyfriend and lived only a few blocks south. He was a percussionist and played in various Broadway theater orchestras. For the coming year we shared the apartment, we saw little of one another. Mostly when

I wasn't home, a time convenient for Judith, she would pick up her mail and phone messages. There was a barrage of calls with long detailed messages, spoken at a quick theatrical clip. I did not prove apt in taking these accounts, which were all extremely important and I was severely reprimanded for not always getting it all straight. Yet I tried hard.

A week had elapsed since arriving in New York and the next step was to get a job after school so I could support myself. I had wanted to arrive a week before school started to make these arrangements, but my father had insisted that I leave the day before classes began. Again I searched the *New York Times* under 'jobs wanted' this time. A few blocks south from Traphagen, on Broadway, I interviewed at a restaurant that stayed open all night. It was decided that I looked far too frail to carry heavy trays for waitressing, but a hostess position was offered to me and I was to start right away. I was overjoyed.

The coming morning in class, Mrs. Pizzo wasn't pleased at all about my newly acquired job. She insisted it was a restaurant known as 'pick up station' for young women. Only barely did I perceive its meaning. I was to quit that job immediately. So next I worked at Schrafft's Restaurant on 34th Street near Grand Central railroad station on the candy counter in conjunction with the restaurant. It was full of delectable treats and proved to be a busy place. A bonus to the job was that we were fed and so I had one good meal a day. Predictably, each night an older gray haired man, immaculately dressed in a business suit, stopped by to purchase some sweets. He always insisted that I wait on him and he always exchanged a few kind words with me. He called me *Pygmalion*. With a friendly twinkle he offered that he was waiting for me to grow up.

Again concerned, Mrs. Pizzo got into the act of finding me

more suitable work. The school office had received notice for two bridal designer trainees in Astoria, Long Island. Betty, a fellow classmate and I were sent out for an interview to Correale's Bridal Shop, which entailed a long complicated subway and then elevated train ride. Pete Correale was middle aged and the most charming owner - designer of the successful shop. His nieces worked in sales and along with the many seamstresses, all spoke Italian. Betty and I were outsiders in this conclave. I could draw, the only one besides Pete, and that immediately put me into the elevated position of working directly with the brides. I loved working with the brides, and as I was informed, a wedding is a woman's most important day and to please her beyond measure was my first obligation. I learned quickly to also please the nieces, since no outsider held a job for long at Pete Correale's. I would bring sample gowns for the brides to try on, and from various designs I would make an attractive sketch collaborating all their ideas. I would pencil in notes on fabric, beadwork and accessories and then the charming maestro would appear to discuss prices and a fitting schedule. A custom-made gown with elaborate beadwork design might keep the seamstresses working for weeks. So each time I sold a gown Pete made a cheery announcement of it and spirits ran high. I sold many gowns. The nieces let me be, stayed out of my way, and Pete showed his appreciation by having a cup of cappuccino waiting for me after school, and often there would be an Italian sweet roll left as well. When Pete was especially pleased, a big stocky man, he'd pounce onto one of those long worktables the seamstresses worked on and sounded off an operatic tune. He attended opera school and sometimes a classmate was visiting and there would be an ecstatic duet. It was a happy time for me until the end of my school program. Betty complained about hauling the heavy bridal gowns about, although she was built much stronger than I was, and she claimed the nieces were picking on her and I was given preferential work of sketching. She didn't stay long. I did mind the extra two subway tokens each day I had to spend, but nothing could be done about that.

Judith was going through a traumatic time in her life. I learned how demanding the acting profession was. In the most positive elated spirit she would rehearse long difficult passages. I admired her devotion, her brilliance. Then she didn't get the part she thought she was made for. I had never witnessed such despair. She would cry, she would scream out her frustrations and I knew nothing to console her. Her deep depressions affected me as well. After those rare nights she spent at our apartment, the next morning I would make her breakfast. A soft-boiled egg, toast and coffee. I would set the table nicely with the few belongings we shared. Most of all in my innocent ways, I tried to cheer her about the brighter tomorrows.

Judith was a late night person and didn't like to rise early, but on those mornings of our breakfasts she got out of bed and faced me in her nightgown, sitting across from one another at our small table with the only two chairs. Judith smiled happily as we would relate to one another our latest happenings. I was not lonely. In class all day and following I worked at Correale's Bridal Shop five evenings, and all day Saturdays. Sundays I would do my homework and clean our apartment. Every moment was counted for. Judith had taken a part time job as secretary working for a publisher, she did some commercials on TV and also modeled for fashion illustrators. We met all our expenses. During our infrequent meetings, she decided on taking advantage of my accent, just in case she had a role that required her to play a foreigner. So endlessly she mimicked me. I do not know if she ever had occasion to use my accent.

June 20th was my nineteenth birthday. Judith and Michael decided to spend some time with me that day. Jointly they collaborated on a poem. It was a birthday poem depicting my now mature age of nineteen and insisting that I was now all grown up. I sincerely appreciated their poem and their confidence of my being all grown up. I did not feel grown up from one day to the next. There was so much to know and to learn living in New York City. I loved being there. I would take small steps at a time. I would work hard but also enjoy what life had to offer. Yes, I hungered for life.

My mother had emigrated to Canada where her oldest sister Eva lived. I had seen my mother only once in five years. She did not write often. I had not intended to return to my father and stepmother's home, but I wanted to write them this last letter. I stated the latest developments since leaving for school. All was managed well. I thanked them for having accommodated me in their home. I thanked them for allowing me to finish high school. Most of all I wanted to express my gratitude for allowing me to prepare for a dream, enabling me to attend fashion design school and to commence my career.

Mornings I would depart after breakfast with a prepared sandwich for lunch. Into my round blue hatbox I would pack supplies I expected to use for classes plus my lunch. Down the steps of five floors, I energetically left 82nd Street, headed thirty blocks straight south on Broadway for Traphagen. This I did to save the 15 cent token, since I already had to spend two tokens to get me to and from work in Astoria, Long Island. I walked rain or shine or snow. I was slender and felt physically fit. At times I would be stopped and asked if I was a model or a dancer. I suppose this was because of my slender build and the hatbox models were known to carry. Bemused I would fend off offers for modeling engagements.

Our beloved teacher Mrs.Pizzo wasn't well. All day she would carry about a cup of strong smelling black coffee. She too smelled of coffee when she addressed each of us on our individual design samples. Her husband was at the painful end stage of cancer, and she stayed up all night comforting him. Often Mrs. Pizzo was absent. I had sewn for as long as I can remember and all projects seemed easy for me. So I was helping my classmates with their sample and design problems, which endeared me to Mrs. Pizzo. Sketch classes were easy as well since I had worked at an advertising studio, and my illustrations were already published in newspapers and some magazines. Life drawing classes were extremely boring as we had the same old male model who showed little sign of vitality. Here too I had experience working from the nude figure in evening courses I had taken at Rochester College. Because of a drinking problem, something that was incomprehensible for me to understand at the time, this instructor was more absent than present.

Here too I was assisting the other first-to third-year students. I had worked so hard saving up the tuition to attend this school, and although proud and happy in giving assistance, I had hoped to learn more. I could attend school for only one year, instead of the three years requirement, so I intended to gain as much knowledge as possible in these open classes, where all students worked at their own pace and capabilities. Students had come from many parts of the world, Puerto Rico, Mexico, Egypt, Iran, Japan and Germany. I learned it was also called a finishing school. Many students were well to do and after completing classes, they were not expected to work.

The class I did really enjoy, aside from form-designing,

draping muslin, was pattern making. We created a personal slop-
er, mathematically ruled out on paper of our own measurements
and other complex design projects. It was technical, challenging,
and the teacher close to her retirement was most competent.

If not taken while working on some project, we enjoyed
lunch in Mrs. Traphagen's penthouse garden. Mrs. Traphagen,
the owner - director of this fashion enterprise, was a tall stately
lady with white hair. She wore the same black dress during all my
stay. She did not seem easily approachable, yet she allowed us to
lunch in her garden which was filled with potted plants and flowers, and pigeons would flutter about galore. Most of all I enjoyed
the panoramic views of the Manhattan skyline, the busy streets,
happenings in the East and the Hudson River. We would cluster
about small round metal tables, and I felt at peace.

I had made a few friends but had little time to socialize.
Gabriele came from Germany for a couple of semesters and as I
later discovered she lived in a castle. She came to my small apartment and taught me to cook some simple meals, mostly things
stirred into a large frying pan. I did not know how to cook. My
stepmother had been a very good cook, but I was destined to do
the cleaning. In turn I helped Gabriele with her drawings. Some
of the students, who had time and the means for frivolous matters, cut snips off my hair and then had their hairdressers match
my hair color. I was amused.

Close to the Christmas holidays I received an anonymous letter. In the letter it stated that it was observed that I had been
an industrious student and helpful to my classmates. A gift of a
$100. was included. I was elated. Up to that time I was able to
manage on my small salary, pay Judith, who took care of the bills.
Yet I struggled paying for class materials, but that too somehow
got worked out. What would I spend such a huge sum of money

on? Most of the students left home for the holidays. My father had invited me for Christmas break but did not include a train fare. As it turned out, my two young half brothers became ill and the family did not celebrate. So I used this unexpected gift to visit my mother, my sister Elfi who finally joined her in Toronto, and my Aunt Eva. It was a joyful reunion.

It was a long train ride from New York City to Toronto. I had designed and sewn a winter coat, gray checked wool with a large collar that served as hood as well and in the latest fashion. We acquired exquisite unusual fabrics in the small basement fabric shops on the Lower East Side at reasonable prices. No one wore a coat like mine. Along with a few other garments I had designed as class projects and updated my wardrobe with, I felt elegant and exuberant in my youth.

Both my mother and aunt had aged. Both had been strong, large built and attractive women. Now their shiny black hair had turned a lusterless gray, and their faces looked sallow. I recalled my mother always managed to wear new fashionable outfits, and she always had her hair done regularly at the beauty parlor and used bright red lipstick. She had been considered a very attractive woman. *Tante* Eva, who had never married, arrived first in Canada and worked at the homeless shelter as a cook. I did not know her to be a chef, but she was much appreciated in her capacity to prepare huge pots filled with exotic soups and stews. Anything at hand found their way into those pots and they were always emptied. I visited her once at the shelter but declined a bowl of the day's specialty. *Tante* Eva knew how to vibrate the violin as passionately as a gypsy did and she could also play the flute. She had more of a free spirit than any of her dozen siblings and therefore was little appreciated.

My mother found employment looking after a young boy and

doing domestic work. The little boy had fallen out of the first story window but wasn't harmed. She then did housekeeping at the hospital. I tried to draw a portrait of my mother in pencil, as I was in the habit of carrying sketching materials with me wherever I went. Physically she had changed so much. I had been trained to draw anything at the advertising studios. Yet I could not make a good drawing of my mother or of my sister.

My younger sister by four years now seemed very grown up. Being younger and separated from one another much of our lives, we were not close. Elfi was of my height and physical build but much stronger. Her hair and complexion were darker than mine. She was apt to get into trouble often and so required most of my mother's attention. In temperament she was stronger willed as well. She had few friends as things had to be done her way. Although I was brought up that the older sibling and oldest of the cousins would give in to maintain peace, at times I would stand firm. Early on by looks and raw maturity she would also be estimated as the older of us, which did not please her. Elfi had blossomed into young womanhood too early.

By necessity my mother had to come to Canada first and saved the fare for Elfi to join her later. She had stayed with my grandmother who could assert little authority over her. Meanwhile my father gave little or no financial and moral support. Much later in life, a wise old childless friend would volunteer from his observations that "children grow up despite their parents." Not totally comprehending, sadness and guilt filled my heart at that reunion. We were sisters but raised at opposite spectrums. We each were painfully scarred by our early life exposures and we would carry those scars for the rest of our years. Yet I felt I broke those chains, in the most naïve fashion, carved a path that determined the rest of my life.

The apartment they all shared was a one flight walk up in the business section of Toronto, not yet the metropolis Toronto it was to become. Small as the domicile would seem, our spirits ran high at being reunited. We toured the city, visited a museum and walked the main streets. I was fascinated with the outdoor markets, where one could buy live chickens, geese, turkeys, fish and an abundance of fresh vegetables, dried goods and clothing. Practically anything was for sale when Toronto yet seemed like a provincial town.

14 Recollections of New York City c

DURING THE COLD months there wasn't much heat ascending from the basement boiler room to our brownstone, fifth floor apartment. Judith eloquently put in her petition for more heat. To no avail. This seemed to be a common phenomena in the city's upper floor dwellings. The rare times Judith spent at our apartment, she expected the heat and comfort we paid for.

It was the slow season at Coreale's Bridal Shop. Most of the seamstresses and nieces had been laid off. I supposed since I needed the income most, Pete kindly kept me on. I was to decorate the walls with large illustrations of the various bridal gowns he had created and all drawing materials he supplied. Eagerly I set to work. Pete's opera friend, Melvin, started showing interest in me and one night insisted taking me home. I pleaded that it had been a long day and the subway ride would take him out of his way, but nothing could persuade him of his intentions. Finally, he huffed up the five floor walk-up. Inside the apartment, he promptly, without ceremony stripped and placed his nude self onto the couch. What to do? Already I had faced another nude male in life drawing class that day. Incessantly I talked about my roommate returning any minute, and she slept on that couch. I glanced about the living room, surely there wasn't much to suggest of another's person living here. Calmly he responded that he was tired and expected to stay the night. He may have gotten weary of not getting any sexual responses to his exposed efforts. It seemed eternity, but he did leave and of course Judith did not appear. Pete must have heard about his friend's unsuccessful venture. So when Melvin showed up in the evenings and followed me about, Pete would confidentially help me depart early and quietly through the back door.

On one occasion Rollie Zavada came to pick me up Saturday after work. He looked dashing, driving up to the shop in his convertible, a red Alpha Romero sports car. As Rollie's stately figure climbed out of this Italian status symbol, Pete spotted him first. It was closing time and we girls took turns cleaning the shop. It was my day to sweep the floor. Pete made the connection quickly that I had a suitor. Instantly he dashed for the corn stalk broom and grabbed it out of my hands. "Barbara, you don't do this kind of work," and he proceeded with the sweeping. I made the introduction, and with the maestros most charming smile, he insisted on my leaving early.

On other occasions, Kozo Miyake, another Rochester friend introduced by a Japanese girlfriend, came for visits. He was quiet and refined and taller than most Japanese I had met. As a full time student at Rochester University, he worked towards his doctorate in physics. We ate at Japanese restaurants, sometimes with his friends, and we went to classical concerts. Life was exciting. I fell in love. He instructed me in the oriental ways. I was concerned about lacking a formal education but he assured me that character was most important. "Education means just a cloth of our spirit. People dressed in most luxurious robes and if they have a poor body it means nothing. A beautiful body will look splendid even in modest dress."

His family were Kyoto landholders. Both his father and his sister were medical doctors. To Kozo my interest in art seemed like an acceptable pasttime, perhaps in the future translating it into flower arranging. At the time I did not know my passion for fine art but I had worked so hard to study fashion designing and art, and I planned on working in this chosen field. As his wife I could not work. His sister was openly hostile to the idea of bringing me to Japan. It was considered a scandal to find one's own mate. Tsuneko's marriage was arranged. She married into a family with many servants and lived in her husband's home. Happiness was never discussed. She did not respond to her brother's letters asking for our support. Kozo shared his fear that the family scandal might affect his sister's marriage, and that she might get divorced if we were to marry. Professor Miyake expected him to get over his rebellious ways, undoubtedly brought on by his American associations. Quietly Kozo persisted in wanting to choose his own bride. He knew that when he returned in his early thirties with his degree, ready to resume his research at Kyoto University, his father would arrange a marriage. His parents were distant relatives, adopted by the childless landholder and later married to one another.

Gabriele spent more time at my apartment. The second semester was coming toward an end. She was returning to Germany, and it was the end of my schooling at Traphagen as well. This was all I could afford. I had fitted three years into these two semesters, but since I didn't pay for the full course, I did not get the credit either. There were fashion competitions city wide, and we all participated. I helped Gabriele with the drawings for the competition. It was important for her to return home with a prize, so she prepared many designs. I only submitted one design, and it won New York City's 'first fashion prize' with a cash bonus. Graduating with a diploma but at the top of my class with straight A's, I hoped this would help me in finding work in the competitive fashion world.

Woman's Wear Daily was New York's fashion newspaper, called the 'Bible of the Fashion Industry.' I had set aside time to prepare

Winning NYC first fashion prize, 1959

a portfolio of sketches, which I hoped would appeal to the directors of the fashion houses. We all searched the WWD Classified Jobs Wanted ads. It struck me that for the year's fashion graduates city wide, very few positions were available. Furthermore during the couple of interviews I was lucky to obtain, everyone asked for a minimum of five years designing experience. I had considered it an advantage of having worked as an illustrator and for a year as bridal designer during school. So I made an appointment at an employment office serving the industry. I looked well groomed, wore a fashionable outfit, and I was proud to present my portfolio. The middle aged interviewer patiently viewed my portfolio. He opened the door wide of the small office then got out his tape measure. He offered, "I have an opening for a designer's model." Then he proceeded to take measurements of my bust, waist and hips. He said at 5' 6" I was a bit short and my hips were too wide. He suggested I go home and put on a tight girdle and then the same afternoon present myself to the newly opened fashion house of Burke-Amey. It may be a way to break in.

During school I had led a spartan life and now my slender build was to be an advantage. This fashion house had its beginning in a somber looking brownstone, first floor apartment off

Central Park West. Ronald Amey was short, slight, balding, and the genius of the firm. Burke provided the financial backing. Ron studied my portfolio with interest and only much later admitted that I proved talented. Of course I was there for a different purpose. Nicole, an attractive but robust seamstress with a strong French accent, was called to assist me. Behind a room divider I had to undress, tight girdle and all, to be fitted into an even tighter bracelette, a tight fitting undergarment. When Nicole brusquely tied me up I thought I would pass out. She then fitted me into a most exquisite long gown. Ron Amey critically passed around me, tucked at some folds and stepped back to appraise his creation on me. He commented, "a bit short," then with a smile, "you will do." That was my start as a designer's personal model.

Ron Amey did the designing and cutting of garments in the evenings after we departed. This was in preparation for his first major fashion show. There were only six seamstresses at the start, all foreigners, and mostly French was spoken. He produced exclusive evening gowns in the $3,000 to $4,000 range with a couple of simple black bread- and-butter dresses starting at $300. It was 1960. When not tied into the straight jacket of a bracelette or trying on various partly completed gowns, I too was sewing on these gowns of rare internationally imported fabrics. First, I started out just hemming skirts but quickly I was promoted to the various haute couture practices under the expert tutelage of our Paris trained head seamstress. In this one room with only a small window we worked in absolute silence as Ron Amey drank black coffee, smoked cigarettes and just observed us all day long, always a step ahead of our sewing projects. On occasion the fashion editors of *Vogue* or *Harper's Bazaar* would visit, and Ron Amey was aflutter. Painfully strapped into the bracelette, Nicole was not gentle, I would be asked to try on various gowns. Under the master's direction, I pirouetted before these powerful ladies and stepped close for their inspection. I was sensitive and shy and did not enjoy these ladies fingering my body. It was my duty though to show off most advantageously these beautiful creations. Their compliments could mellow our stern boss into elated gestures and a higher pitched voice. On another matter, the only Singer sewing machine used by all of us caused much consternation. The machine broke down often, and Ron Amey could be angry. He had no difficulty using it, and he refused to buy a new one. As a young child I had learned to use my mother's foot pedaled Singer sewing machine, and so I had no difficulty with this machine. When he said "Barbara has no problem with it," it did not endear me to my fellow workers.

Arriving home late one night, I found the apartment in disarray. The skylight in the bathroom was shattered. Chips of glass and dirt apparently from the roof were everywhere. Clothes out of our dressers were scattered all about. Panicking, something I rarely did, I called Judith at Michael's. Both arrived immediately and together we assessed the damage. Judith's hi - fi and sewing machine were gone. So was her diamond bracelet, but a rhinestone bracelet was left behind by obviously professional thieves. I also lost the only gift I recalled receiving from my father, a Swiss watch for high school graduation with *Tante* Gertrud frowning, my alarm clock and the few pieces of jewelry I possessed, a heart shaped gold medallion that could be opened, a farewell gift of my grandmother when I departed for the USA, the piece I treasured most. The feeling of intrusion into our private domain mostly concerned us both. The police were called but did not arrive until a week later. There were too many burglaries, the policeman responded, and they had more important matters to tend to. Judith as usual was more emotional but eloquent. She and

Michael incessantly probed me about the happening. Such a valuable piece as a diamond bracelet should have been kept in a safe, I thought but didn't verbalize it. With our landlord Judith was persistent about installing iron bars beneath the repaired skylight. He did not comply, and we decided it was time to move and go our separate ways.

This happened during my first week of full-time employment. Not awakening to my alarm, I was late every single morning as I timidly entered the studio to Ron Amey's sinister glance. On my first pay day I immediately invested in a new alarm clock I had already picked out. Not having time for lunch in our half hour break, I quickly picked up an ice cream cone before I hurried back. Ron Amey looked aghast. "You can not afford to eat that," as he gestured to the cone, then to the waste basket. I weighed a mere one hundred pounds. While in school I could not afford to eat and now with a full-time salary I wasn't allowed to eat.

I moved to a single room in an apartment house a few blocks north to the corner of Riverside Drive and the park. It was a small room painted grass green, not my choice, but clean. There was a cot, dresser, one chair, a small under-the-counter refrigerator, two burner hot plate and a small washstand with hot and cold water. The apartment was located on the third floor, but the bathroom with shower was on the second floor and much in demand. Once a week we would receive clean sheets and towels. I enjoyed the proximity of the narrow park which extended up half of Manhattan Island to the George Washington Bridge. There I could walk, the Hudson River teeming with boating activity for many miles. I was to stay here for another year so filled with activities that little time was spent in the room, and I could afford it.

An imposing brand new brass shield was displayed at the

corner of 57th street and 5th Avenue inscribed *Burke-Amey Haute Couture*. More seamstresses were hired as we filled a spacious room on the second floor with many large windows flooding in daylight. The show room was equally as large, elegant with hardwood floors, large mirrors covering the walls. There was a wooden platform used as stage, where I now modeled the exquisite Amey creations for the magazine editors and clients who ordered gowns in their respective sizes. Viewing myself in those fabulous attires and in those enormously sized mirrors with bright reflections of windows and studio lights, I would have never dreamed of looking as beautiful. I was beautiful. Models 5'8" - 5'10" were to do the seasonal fashion shows and magazine photo promotions.

The workroom had long tables for the seamstresses to comfortably sew separate parts of the garments, each to her ability. I no longer helped with the sewing. I'd been promoted to do the cutting of the garments for which Ron Amey made the paper or muslin patterns. At the far end of the studio I had my own large cutting table. To provide so many seamstresses with work, I had to be swift, and I worked much overtime. Also the assignment of various garments or part of them was delegated to me. We had a new, middle aged woman sent by an agency. What she lacked in experience, she compensated for in good will. I patiently worked with her, just as I had helped my fellow classmates with their sewing projects. She confided in me that she had been a prostitute all her life and earnestly was seeking new work and a new life. She had enjoyed sewing but the years of harsh living had taken a toll. Apparently she did not know how to look appropriate and sadly she had lost the dexterity, especially for working on such fine and complex sewing projects. I'd give her simple hems to do, I patiently guided her, but my good will was not sufficient, and I was asked, for the first time in my life, to fire a person. She took it well. She had faced up to many failures.

Of my former classmates I inquired as to their fates. Gabriele had returned to Germany and expected to marry. My friend Bunny stayed home to work up beautiful wardrobes for her country club social life. Some were married and were starting families. The majority though worked as secretaries, hoping still to break into the fashion field later. Two of the young men with financial backing had a private clientele. One man I accidentally discovered was designing for the Canadian Shakespearean Theater. There just weren't enough jobs for all of the graduates city wide or nationally.

Still life was good. I felt at peace. For just this moment challenges had been met. I felt at home and at ease in this metropolis. Excitement overcame me, a joy felt as deep pain - as I partook the throb of this energizing city. "Survival of the fittest," and I sustained. What brought me here? Incredibly having survived to experience the present. The birth of an idea came upon me as I elatedly stepped in a dreamlike trance through this asphalt jungle called New York. I was going to write an account. I lived in the present and would continue to do this. Always keeping the door shut, tight, to my earliest memories.

14 Recollections of New York City d

WORKING FOR SO many hours overtime at Burke-Amey's made me decide it was time to start something new or the job would devour me. I worked six to seven days, and late into the nights before our first fashion show. I was on a small salary, but always having lived frugally, I was able to put a small amount of my earnings into savings each week. Our first fashion show was proclaimed a huge success by the media. We employees partook in the merriment. I had one or two glasses of champaign, but not being accustomed to alcohol, I barely got myself home. I then made the decision to make the time to start at the highly acclaimed Art Students League part-time, evenings. We did not work for credit or degrees but rather chose a subject and some of the world renowned artists - instructors. George Grosz taught life drawing. He was a German expatriate and had been threatened by Hitler for his well known satirical drawings, making light of the Third Reich and its populace. Judging his well publicized stylized renderings, I found it astounding what a fine draftsman and teacher he was. I loved the aura of distinct League smells, oil paint and turpentine. There was a *laissez-faire* ambiance which I had not encountered before. I quickly made associations with the students. As well I started part-time modeling which paid for the classes. I too loved the involvement of the paintings and sculptures being created. If I had a wish, I would have wanted to be the wife of an artist and contribute to his inspiration - for him to create. Those days it was not easily conceivable for a woman to aspire to be a painter herself. Women weren't numerous at the

125

League and most took drawing or designing courses.

As a group we met at the League's coffee shop before classes. This immigrant, George Grosz, to us seemed bigger than life, a real hero during World War II, who had risked his life by exposing his political feelings through his now well publicized caricatures in water color and pen and ink drawings. He received ultimate respect and commanded a large student following. I was fortunate to partake in his instructions and lectures before he passed away. After evening classes, groups of students congregated late into the night in favorite haunts close to the League over coffee or beer. On paper napkins we drew caricatures of one another, a Grosz inspiration, to be taken as compliments. No one seemed to be able to make a good caricature of my features. Discussions of books read but banned in the USA, like Lady Chatterley's Lover preoccupied us for evenings. Grosz's political exploits were a recurring topic. This too was my introduction to classic black and white European and Russian classical films. Money was scarce to all of us, and income, either by family allowances or part-time jobs, kept our heads above water. But we did indulge in Ingmar Bergman's films, as well as Fellini's and with awe witnessed the Eisenstein film series offered in the Museum of Modern Art, to which we all had membership. My introduction to Charley Chaplin movie shorts was free of charge in a Greenwich Village coffee house.

Weekends we would meet to view gallery exhibits on 57th Street and upper Park Avenue. Exhibits were all free at the Metropolitan, Guggenheim, Whitney and beloved to us all, The Museum of Modern Art. I hungered for knowledge. Abstract Expressionism was the rage. I experimented with my first humble abstract drawings in pencil, pen and brush in india ink. With the influx of European master artist and artisan immigrants after

World War II, who settled in New York City, the world art center shifted from Paris to New York. This new immigrant talent produced such renowned painters as Hans Hoffmann, William de Kooning and George Grosz who made New York their creative base. The climate was ripe for such innovators as Jackson Pollock, Franz Kline, Mark Rothko, Clifford Still, Louis Morris, Robert Motherwell, Helen Frankenthaler and Theodoros Stamos who challenged the current art establishment. Stamos was also part of what was called the Irascibles with whom I later studied. It was exciting to witness this great transformation and to be part of it. Incessantly we combed the galleries and museums for the new art forms. We witnessed, we experimented, we lived art.

Rarely did I see Judith now. She did more television shorts and was now ready to delegate some of her modeling assignments to me. It meant posing for individuals and as well groups of illustrators. The work paid very well. It was physically strenuous standing up and holding long poses in high heels under hot fluorescent spot lights, but I was appreciated and much in demand. Money flowed in and I was cautious to put it away safely for whatever coming venture.

I was the only one in our group of student artists who had a full-time job, plus with the extra modeling income, soon enough I was asked to make loans, $5.00 a clip. I loaned out money but it never was returned to me, and I was too shy to ask for it. So I let it be known that I had purchased a portable Singer sewing machine and that I needed to make payments. It was partially true, but the scheme worked.

At Burke-Amey's there were no changes. I worked hard for a small salary and much overtime as assistant to supply work for the many seamstresses, and I wasn't paid overtime. I figured, perhaps it wasn't coincidence that we were all foreigners, hard working and too timid to speak up for ourselves and our rights. It was time to move on and now to take a stand and truly try to survive in the tough garment district, meaning, survival of the fittest in the renown fashion industry. I worked at Jonathan Logan junior sportswear and several other jobs successively in sportswear and day wear as fashion sketcher or assistant. This meant gaining experience and insight into the workings of mass produced 7th Avenue fashion merchandise.

Our League group now discussed exploring the European continent for an extended stay to personally experience Old World art at its roots. A new dream came to mature. Everyone was on some kind of a savings program. Individually some were inclined to plan time in Italy, Austria, Holland, Scandinavia, the near East or Israel, but a stay in Paris would be incorporated by every one, however short.

My father had to agree to become a US citizen before accepting a position in America. He and his family promptly, after the five-year residence, became citizens just before I departed for New York. Citizenship for me had not been an urgent matter then, but my roots in the USA had deepened. Family and friends in Germany seemed distant. If I were to travel to Europe, I would certainly like the option to return to the United States. It now seemed a simple decision. So I applied for citizenship and prepared to take the exam. With a busy work schedule and social life, I heard and saw less of Kozo. He was deeply upset with my life style. Long letters bemoaned the fact that I had clearly gone off the track. There was also much opposition from his family to bring me to Japan. Even worse for me to contemplate becoming a US citizen. Anti-US feelings were still strong in Japan, and he hoped as a German I was more acceptable to his family. For me the decision seemed right to attain US citizenship. Already I had suffered much not being accepted in my father's household, being on foreign soil. I did not want to repeat this painful experience in the oriental culture, married to a man who was obedient to his strong willed parents and sister.

I was well prepared for the citizenship exam. The appointment was set. That morning I had completely lost my voice, at best I could only croak and it was too late to cancel. My two required witnesses were Judith and Mark, my good friend from the League. By subway we headed for lower Manhattan to City Hall. A great many people were present and there was much confusion as to where the exams were held and the signing of certificates. Some of the applicants brought whole families as witnesses and there were many children underfoot jumping about. All this worked to my benefit as we were quickly expedited. Of all the material I studied conscientiously, only a few questions were asked and I did manage to coax out the few words. With the signing of my citizenship papers and reciting the Pledge of Allegiance, I received my congratulations from the officer, Judith and Mark. We each then parted our way. At work the reason for my tardiness quickly spread about and with my sore throat I had to accept a drink and more congratulations. By mail shortly afterwards, Governor Nelson Rockefeller too sent his congratulations. So now I was a citizen of the United States and free to travel the far corners of the world and then be able to return home when I wished.

My plans were set for a one-year return to Europe. I booked passage on a small ocean liner, the *SS Hanseatic*, with an anticipated journey of ten days. I was going to bid farewell to my Canadian family. On the long ride to LaGuardia airport the taxi driver addressed me as Greta Garbo, perhaps because of my German accent and mystique. I felt indeed honored. Kozo had not taken my US citizenship well. He had not completed his doctorate but was planning to leave for Japan as well.

I made plans to visit Toronto before my departure. Kozo and I met at Buffalo airport which was on the way. We toured Niagara Falls, wrapped in yellow raincoats as we passed beneath the falls, getting chilled and fully soaked. We met, not really comprehending or accepting that this would be for the last time. Each of us carried deep pain, barely conceiving the majesty of the falls under whose cool spray we walked on this hot summer day. Kozo kept reassuring me, reassuring himself, that he would win over his father. He had saved up my fare and in a year I was to join him in Japan. We would stay in touch while I traveled Europe. We were not totally aware at that time that my decision to return to Europe meant that my life's choice had been made.

My mother had meanwhile made an improvement in her life by becoming a caretaker in a private home of a bachelor with his young daughter on the outskirts of Toronto. She and *Tante* Eva met me at the airport but Elfi was absent. My mother looked distressed. We took a ride to the hospital. Elfi, despondent, was lying on a cot, facing the wall in the hallway. She had taken an overdose of sleeping pills. My mother not speaking the language had Mr. Radford, her employer, call the ambulance. Anger surged within me. I had a better command of English and I demanded to speak with the doctor immediately. Why wasn't my sister in a hospital room? The hospital supervisor explained patiently that it was a case of suicide and with no insurance a patient would be allowed to stay in the hallway for a short while.

Why did this happen? I too reproached myself as it occurred at the time of my arrival, with my spirits running high of this incredible feat of returning to Europe. I had paid my dues with hard work, discipline and foresight. Elfi could not compete. Not yet.

We had the same genes but raised in different environments with different expectations. I realized my father had to deal with many problems as a new immigrant, raising a family and homesickness - not being where he wanted to be. In my anger I reproached him for the negligence of his daughter. My father did not contribute financial support for my sister in Germany or thereafter in Canada. After all he took care of me. Responsibility split? My mother was not emotionally strong and with only a grade school education, she was not in any way prepared to deal with life's challenges. Yet the immigrant spirit came through in making a path of her own with gradual slight improvements. What made me strong I wondered. Perhaps by hard knocks of immigrant life?

Reminiscing our last meeting. Elfi sat at the Radford's dining room table with books and notepapers laid about. Some contemporary tunes were blasting out. I sat across the table from her and talked softly about the music being too loud to concentrate, especially studying for exams. This had been her freshman year. I talked about how important it had been for me to finish high school. It would open doors in later life. Good grades in high school might mean going to college later - perhaps. It could be an option. The music continued to blast and Elfi looked defiant as she concentrated on the songs. My mother wept softly.

On my return trip to New York I had promised Rollie Zavada to stop by for a day. I did not harbor fond memories of Rochester. My father and family had since moved to Chicago. It proved to be the cheerful respite I needed. Rollie was always happy and knew the secret of creating for himself interesting pastimes and he enjoyed his work at Eastman Kodak. Although he very gradually worked part-time on his masters degree, it was important for him to play and have fun. He was thirteen years older than I was, and with slightly graying hair, he seemed to me incredibly mature. He produced a Rochester newspaper front page feature article depicting him on Valentines Day "the most eligible bachelor of the year." Indeed, women were pursuing him and he was happy to talk about it. We walked the lilac gardens close to his apartment and drove about town in his red convertible sports car. He was ready to settle down but I still needed to experience Europe to understand myself better and to find out where I belonged. He too thought that I needed this experience to sort out things in my life that were to me not yet totally comprehensible.

I had met Bunny McAlpine at Traphagen. Older and with a family, she wanted to learn to create a wardrobe for her lavish lifestyle. From a modest background she had married well. Golf and the country club were her passion. Just before I planned on leaving for Europe, she invited me to spend the weekend at her gorgeous home in luscious Summit, New Jersey. As golf was her passion, everything evolved around it. With Kim, her lovely lithe daughter of about ten with a head of golden brown tight curls, we were to amuse ourselves at the country club pool while Bunny persued her passion.

Bunny, extremely fashion conscious, who bought exotic fabrics from all over the world and had some gowns internationally designed for her or some created herself, abandoned her game like the rest of the golfers to hurry over to the pool to witness 'the first bikini.' Not only the golfers but the country club personnel lined the fence and gawked in utter disbelieve. Country club rules are stringent and obeyed religiously. To Bunny the rules were divine. Ominously I heard Bunny's deep raspy voice calling among the multitude, "Barbara." Three decades later, when daughter Erika and son-in-law John briefly visited Bunny on their way to a friend's wedding in Westport, Connecticut, over lunch at the same country club, the old tale was recounted. "To think it was my houseguest, your mother, sporting that bikini."

Just days remained until my departure. Frugally once again I had saved up every dime, living modestly, preparing for life's coming venture. I sold the used bicycle. In addition to my two suitcases and two hatboxes, I now also acquired a wardrobe trunk. There wasn't time to pack as I had a day job until the day I left. Evenings and Saturdays I modeled to earn extra income for the long journey. I gave notice on the various jobs. At the studio where I modeled for groups of illustrators, I had to stand on a platform in the center of a large studio, well lit with hot spotlights burning down on me, while the artists sat in a full circle around me. I had not been paid for some time. The director explained, I was his model most in demand and he wanted me to pose until the last evening before my boat was to depart. After that last session I would be paid. So with aching bones, cramping muscles and my full paycheck, late that last evening I returned for the last time to the grass green sliver of a room to start packing for this most adventurous journey of my life.

15 Experiencing the European Continent a

SURROUNDED BY A circle of fashion illustrators, center stage, I posed late into the night at my final modeling job on fashionable 57th Street in New York City. I seemed to be the most popular model for this group, and I would only obtain my full pay if I worked until the last night before my European departure. Tired and with muscles cramping from holding long poses under hot spotlights, I hurriedly completed packing that night.

The coming morning I left on a small modest ocean liner, the North German *SS Hanseatic*, mainly with students either

Group gathering on the *SS Hanseatic* crossing
the Atlantic for Europe 1960

returning to Europe after their completed degrees or Americans planning to study abroad. It was a vivacious group full of anticipation of the sometimes unknown. We did not look for a restful journey as many fun activities such as games and dances were offered. Meals were modest and not our prime concern. My cabin mates were two students and an older extremely fat lady who took command as our cabin mother. We were a happy cabin family.

Starting that same afternoon on the sportsdeck, a bottle of whisky made the rounds as we sang German and American folksongs, danced, flirted until four or five in the mornings. Midsummer 1960, in beautiful weather at high sea no one became sea sick as so many of us had done on my previous sailing over the Atlantic, missing out on first class comfort. This was a meeting of the minds, friendships made with promises of staying in touch forever.

**Self with cousins Laurence and Dagmar Ayling
at Trafalgar Square, London**

THE IMMIGRANT

Half of us departed the *SS Hanseatic* in South Hampton and then proceeded by train to London. We all checked into the Imperial Hotel, took a night walk to Trafalgar Square, the hub of town with fountains and lively discourse and then dined at 3 AM. Bill Farrar, an Australian engineer, who had worked for a year in Canada, came to visit my relatives, god - mother Asta, her husband Jack with my cousins Dagmar and Laurence, whose British accents I absolutely adored. They lived in Essex, Leigh-on-Sea.

Tante Asta was a war bride. She met Jack, a British officer, working as an English and French interpreter. They both loved art dearly but did not choose it as profession. They were married in Rissen at my mother's house. Instead of cake we made a huge jello pudding from *Onkel* Reinhold's US care package and it was a sensation. Embarrassingly it was discovered that I did not speak English and *Onkel* Jack needed *Tante* Asta to translate.

Now we received a warm welcome. I commuted to London taking in the British Fine Arts Museum, Tate Gallery with an exhausting night life, tasting warm ale and experiencing the new and traditional stiff democratic customs. Bill had set out to tour the world before settling down in that far yonder territory, Australia. While crossing the ocean we had not gotten to know each other well, but now, with like intentions, we planned to travel the European continent next summer, camping on a shoestring, as we all needed to watch expenses. Ten-year-old Dagmar was very taken with Bill and promised to marry him if I didn't want to.

The next leg of the journey took me from Marwich on the east coast. I sailed the English Channel for six hours on the crowded *Köningen Wilhelmina*. There was hardly standing room on the overcrowded boat, so I stayed on the restaurant deck, deeply engrossed in Leon Uris' *Exodus*. I was also drawn into an

136

interesting discussion by two Nigerian statesmen of advanced age, one in formal Western clothing and the other wrapped in colorful native robes. We talked politics, race problems, art, and literature. At the end of the journey the statesmen concluded that I was a well educated, wealthy little American girl looking for adventure on the European continent. I had to forego a dinner invitation as my train was to depart the town Hook of Holland for Amsterdam. Diminutive farms spread before us with many water channels passing by peacefully.

Not being accustomed to travel, I had no advance reservations for accommodations in Amsterdam. I went to a small quaint hotel on a narrow side street this busy summer season. All rooms were booked. An Italian girl traveling with her fiancé was also in the waiting line. The kind *concierge* moved some guests and then offered the shy Italian girl and myself to share a room. Tired, we were gratefully ready to slumber off when the only interference was an American soldier, half drunk, passing our door, demanding to see the American girl. A refreshing shower and typical Hollandaise breakfast prepared me for my journey to my former home.

Next, I took the train ride to a much anticipated return to Hamburg. I was happy to stay to myself in a *coup* compartment, and rest. A group of nine Norwegian *Pfadfinder* - boy scouts descended upon me. We had a lively discourse. Accompanied by someone playing guitar, we sang Norwegian and German *Wanderlieder,* folksongs. Arrival into my former home country could not have been more enjoyable. I was ready to move on to Norway with the *Pfadfinder*. In Hamburg, at my departure, many eager hands assisted with the luggage, and we parted with warm farewells.

There was a two-hour wait for the train to Rissen at 6 AM

and then I arrived only to wake my grandmother. Much had changed. With my mother and sister having migrated to Canada, my closest relation was now my grandmother. In those absent seven years she hadn't changed physically or spiritually. She was in her late eighties, her long hair knotted into a bun at the nape of her neck, deep brown with only a few straying gray hairs. She now happily managed the small apartment by herself. It was her custom to walk at least several miles each day in every kind of weather, and I was happy to accompany her on walks that brought memories alive. This two-week stay proved to be totally relaxing from my travels and many late nights and prepared me for the exhausting journey ahead.

Since my departure seven years ago Hamburg and the suburbs were totally rebuilt, and modernized with a clean and affluent look. Rissen had expanded growth of fine villas into the forests and heather flats. Main Street still maintained cobble

Reunion with Hamburg family, myself with grandmother

stones with storefront straw thatched houses, and I noticed some stork nests still artfully nestled near the chimneys. I discovered that I hadn't missed anything these years. The majority of classmates were married or engaged. Fridel learned flower arranging in Switzerland. Hedi, now von Aspern, married a man with a title, who moved into her affluent homestead. I chanced upon her as she was pushing a baby carriage, hurriedly delivering newspapers in Höhnerkamp, for pocket money and she was worried about serving dinner tardy to the homecoming husband. She had always been the biggest girl, but now her once so attractive face had swelled and she only squinted those beautiful blue eyes. She had no time to talk.

Gerlinde and I still felt a bond despite the long separation, and we retraced many of our old walks into the far out country and yonder to the pure white beaches of the Elbe River. We spent time in Hamburg, the stately harbor city restored to its old magnificence. We did the touristy things like taking in the harbor section with infamous St. Pauli, climbed the historic St. Michael, and witnessed the most exciting fireworks accompanied by some classical and modern music in the botanical garden.

Dr. Miyake, from Japan, my friend Kozo's father, attended conferences in England, Scandinavia and Germany, totaling a two month sightseeing round trip of Europe. We spent a memorable day in Hamburg as we easily conversed in English. I translated German for him as we took in an Alster motorboat tour amid all the sailing vessels. Typically his camera rested on me mostly. Afterwards we leisurely drank coffee in the Alster pavillon. We had dinner in the Europaiischer Hof, and a glass of wine kept us talking amiably until midnight. Then he took me to my train for Rissen, and I observed his puzzled and hesitant look as we bid farewell. Kozo had delayed his return to Japan to complete his final exams for his doctorate. He had sent me an enclosed sealed letter for his father, addressed in Japanese, but it did not arrive in time for our meeting. He was asking permission to return with me as his bride. Did fate play its role?

My grandmother and Gerlinde saw me off in Altona for my departure to Berlin. The train was filled to the brim with children and primarily older folks. Passage through the Eastern zone was desolate and sad. I accidentally missed the West station and unintentionally found myself in East Berlin. I had dispersed the last of my money to the luggage carrier. I was famished. The sausage stand and ice cream parlor looked enticing. The exchange was closed, so without any Ostmark I ventured sightseeing East Berlin.

When the exchange reopened I found the course stood I:I. A friendly foreigner explained that the offered rate of exchange was $I to 8 Deutsche Mark in the West. He invited me in his taxi across the border and at the Berliner Thor, under his protection, I wasn't even searched or questioned by the guards. Who was this stranger? A guardian angel? At the Zoobahnhof he helped me with the exchange. To *Tante* Lotte's great surprise, I arrived in an east taxi at her door. First off, *Onkel* Heinz recalled all my youthful misdeeds and their daughter Brigitte had grown into a strapping teenager. They took great pride in their small but tastefully decorated apartment which they had inhabited for twenty years. *Tante* Eva, the oldest and by far the most colorful of the siblings, was much discussed and shredded up wherever I turned, and I as the uninvolved, grew tired of the family quarrels.

I stopped a day in Köln, climbing the Kölner Dom, and then I took a boat trip down the lovely Rhein. I was amused that again I was taken for a rich American girl by a traveling companion. My Traphagen friend Gabriele met me at the Aachen station in her

Volkswagen to take in the views. Ninety percent of the town had been destroyed, although again repaired, many ruins were still visible. At noon we arrived in Stolberg, *Haus Grünthal*, something I was not prepared for, a real castle. We formally lunched in the baroque style dining hall, attended by servants and in the most charming company of her parents. In the afternoon we toured the castle with its magnificent views over the formal gardens. Gabriele's suite was a dream, a formal apartment with a studio. Next we visited the family - owned company, a factory where pharmaceuticals and fine soaps were manufactured. After a formal dinner with the family we talked late into the night in my guest suite, catching up on a year of happenings.

Tante Lenchen and *Onkel* Franz in Antwerp were next on the agenda. After a long separation, we each recognized one another immediately and spent a couple of days visiting the King's palace, one more harbor, and a fine museum of mostly Belgian masters. At night we dined on Belgian specialties, fresh mussels, simply prepared and delicious.

15 Experiencing the European Continent b

Paris I

PARIS WAS MY greatest challenge. I checked into Hotel Brég, in the street of the same name, and took an inexpensive room. Then I looked up my pen pal Chantal Dumont. The family lived above the father's sculpture studio. He had just completed a life-size figure of Brigitte Bardot. This was an awesome, finely anatomized work of the sex symbol, and Monsieur Dumont was proud to walk us around the beautiful figure for appraisal of his masterpiece.

Chantal had been an haute couture fashion model in the house of Balenciaga until her well-publicized automobile accident. On some rare spare moments I had studied French in preparation for this stay. My French at that point was not adequate by far to express what I really wanted to portray but the family was gracious in accepting me. No one spoke English. After a year of correspondence with Chantal from the states, we faced each other for the first time and sized up one another. She was very tall, very slender with short dark red hair, and her face, on which her job depended, was still facing many more cosmetic surgeries before returning to the scrutiny of the public. I received a warm welcome by her family and enjoyed their subsequent dinner invitations. Chantal's facial muscles had been severed so one detected little emotion. We became very good pals about town during my two Parisian stays.

Many Americans and foreigners the world over desired to live in that unique artist heaven - Paris. Accommodations, even for the French, were impossible to obtain. One waited to get married until an apartment or at least servants quarters in stately homes of the major boulevards became available. Many hopefuls did not stay or stayed only until finances ran out. Even a cheap hotel room was too costly for me. At the *Service d'accueil des etudiantes etranges,* so timely, a tiny room was available in an apartment from a widowed *Madam.* There were many locks on the doors and long lists of rules to follow in the kitchen and bathroom. The bare light bulb in my room was of the lowest wattage and I was told to study in the library to conserve electricity and eat in the school cafeteria so as not to use her kitchen. Here I felt more scrutinized than by my stepmother.

My wardrobe trunk and suitcases arrived from Hamburg. I had them forwarded to Paris and stored in *Madam's* basement under her strict supervision. I had to prove to myself that I could stand on my own two feet, further my career and succeed on this continent, alone, barely comprehending the language. At the *maison* of Jacques Heim I interviewed with Monsieur Heim, presenting him with the portfolio I had prepared in New York. He seemed interested but spoke fast and became impatient when I didn't grasp things quickly enough. He sent for Jacques van der Weele, a Dutch design trainee, fluent in many languages including English. Handsome Jacques explained that there was an opening in the tailoring department and Monsieur inquired if I qualified for first - second or third hand. Without hesitation I opted for *premier main* - first hand, believing it was the best hand.

Although I had been first at Traphagen and successfully worked in New York in *haute couture* and 7th Avenue, I was not prepared for *premier main.* The tailoring *atelier,* studio, was divided between French seamstresses and several foreign trainees cultivating fashion experience in this world renown fashion and art capital. There was capable Rudolph Wimmer, an Austrian who expected to open his own design shop in Vienna. Ebbe Gerlam was Swedish, had worked as tailor in London, and was the most experienced of us. Girard, a Lebanese, also wanted to enrich his experience before returning to his homeland. Amiable Jacques, who had been assisting my interview with *Monsieur* Heim was on a stipend and not serious about production of garments since his desire was to become a designer in Holland. I used this as a base, eventually hoping to break into designing and save up for next summer's European safari. Rudolph and Jacques were fluent in French, but I needed to translate in German for Rudolph, as he was the only one who didn't speak English. We worked in a group; we lunched together in a small café inseparable; we shared our spare time exploring Paris and its outskirts.

It became apparent that I lacked knowledge in this *métier* but compensated with good intentions and diligence. The guys, well experienced, inconspicuously aided me step by step in tailoring these magnificent *haute couture* robes and coats. I learned quickly. Now each of the seamstresses had a crush on one of the guys and with misgivings they observed that all their attentions were devoted to the American girl. They resented us speaking another language and also noticed my getting assistance and squealed to *Monsieur* M. the director.

One morning when I was prepared to leave for the studio, *Madame* put forth a ferocious cry. Her é*pingle, pin,* was missing and I had stolen it. *Madame* would call the police if I didn't return her favorite pin that instant. I had never seen that pin and I felt so ill equipped with my limited French to defend myself. Troubled I arrived at work and found the guys sympathetic. Ebbe was soon to depart for Götheburg, Sweden, since he felt he had acquired the knowledge he had been seeking. His apartment was soon to be vacant, so he invited me to move in. After work the guys assisted in retrieving my luggage and wardrobe trunk out of the basement, accompanied by *Madam's* threats and loud screams. Thus we hauled the trunk and luggage to Ebbe's basement. By Paris standards this was a very fine apartment, on the third and top floor overlooking the Bois de Boulogne park. Its main room had a bed and a cot and an adequate kitchen for someone who didn't cook. When it rained, a large pail had to rest on the bed to accommodate the fierce drippings from the ceiling. One took a sponge bath, and the exposed toilet was shared in the hallway. It was a contraption I never planned on getting used to. It was a yard square latrine. One squatted on footrests near the edge of the square. Always, but especially in the cold of winter, while squatting, I thought the devil was going to enter in my interior as a freezing breeze swept up from the hole. Public flush toilets you paid for, more if you washed your hands and used a paper towel. Squatters were free.

Things started to happen career wise. *Echo de la Mode* admired American illustrators, and I started to receive freelance illustration assignments for this magazine, which I worked on nights on my small lap size wooden drawing board. At the House of Dior, I passed some testing of quick sketching from models posing in very beautiful creations that were to be transposed onto pure silk scarves under the name of Dior. I felt in my true element.

Ebbe had been a thoughtful roommate. When he left, my joy as sole apartment dweller was short lived. The landlord wanted to reclaim the apartment for his son who was to return from the Algerian war. Five months had elapsed, and in order to renew my temporary visa, I needed proof of residency. Sadly I had to leave Paris. An artist acquaintance with a studio in the Latin quarter invited me to Picasso's home in the South of France. This and between not very firm job possibilities from either Rome or Copenhagen, I decided rather awkwardly to head north. I bid farewell to the Dumonts. Chantal was deeply upset and refused to understand that it wasn't my choice to delegate that prize of apartment to her and her sister.

On my way to Scandinavia, I detoured over London briefly to visit with Bill and to reconfirm plans for our whirlwind tour of the continent the coming summer. With a group of Australian engineers, he roomed in a large outmoded flat. There was no end to their thoughtful considerations. The first night they served Australian stew, which I so highly praised that they immediately repeated this gourmet meal. I offered to help but all were busily preoccupied in their spacious kitchen. It was plain beef I observed and proudly they proclaimed that everything on hand found itself into the large stew pot. I was only allowed to stand by as these well-trained chefs dumped all vegetables and further ingredients unwashed into the giant pot. I did not much care for their stew afterwards.

In Copenhagen I stayed in a small pension, a room with meals, while I formally interviewed at A/S Frico Modelkjoler. The owner seemed impressed with my design portfolio but showed deep concern about my age, just twenty, claiming I looked more like thirteen. At lunch I ordered a cup of coffee with my sandwich but was given a glass of milk instead. He strongly recommended I return home and grow up some more. No pleading softened his heart. That very night I was firmly encouraged to travel to Berlin to my relatives with a job recommendation to a colleague and major fashion concern.

15 Experiencing the European Continent c

Berlin

ON JANUARY EVENING, 1961, engulfed in heavy fog, our small freighter departed the east coast of Denmark to sail the frigid Baltic Sea for Rostock in the Mecklenburger Bucht, the shortest distance to my destination. My melancholy mood was dispelled by sensing adventures ahead. This trip from the start felt unreal, ghostlike, and I barely remember the details. We undertook this long journey by sea with only four passengers. In dim light, we gathered in a seating cove as the waves tossed us up and about. There was one quiet, old lady with clothes, hair, skin all in gray, a nondescript middle aged man who kept to himself, and another middle aged woman, stout and alone, all with destination Berlin. I had become accustomed to mingling with travelers, and I would have enjoyed some conversation. But this night no one talked to while away the endless night. I tried some small talk but the middle-aged woman seemed to either contradict me or change the conversation.

My mother had talked much about her youth and happy visits to Rostock, sun bathing at the beautiful Baltic beaches where the finest amber was to be found. We disembarked in Rostock harbor in the middle of the night. My luggage was then transported to a waiting train. With a precious hour to spare, adventurously I set out alone in youthful vigor to explore the town I had heard so many tales about.

It was distinctly an East German town. At the train station was only the minimum lighting, one burning light bulb. No one was about, not even a train conductor and the town was dark, everything gray and softly enveloped in fog. I saw no beauty here. The rundown buildings showed decay, with only a bare silhouette to decipher what once had been a majestic town.

I spotted a man alone, perhaps in his late twenties, appearing all gray, wearing a cap with the brim pulled deep over his eyes. I'm sure I must have looked distinctly foreign. My long hair was teased, swept up in the back with pins. I wore a striped jersey wool dress and an expensive suede jacked I had treated myself to in Hamburg. Very slender and always wearing makeup, I did look the part of a well off American. We conversed in German about my wanting to see the town before setting off by train. Streets were cobblestone, and with no lights, they were easy to stumble over. Gallantly the stranger took my arm to guide me, as it is the European custom. Also I became aware that he took a firm hold on my handsome new purse I had bought just before leaving New York. He explained to me some of the sights while I was trying to loosen myself from his grip. I surmised that money is not of much value here but an American passport would be worth a fortune. I had to get away. I pretended to stumble on the cobblestones and broke lose. Luckily I was wearing comfortable walking shoes, rather than my customary spike heels, and I tore off in a fast sprint. I could run. I knew that. The train station was close, and he was close behind me, a good runner too. It was a chase around and between train wagons. I ached in fear. He could easily follow me by the sound of my footsteps. This chase went on for a seemingly endless time, but eventually all out of breath I detected the middle-aged woman waiting for me at the compartment door as we were about to depart. She had wanted to speak to me alone but now it was too late. All she knew was that in a hurry to reach Berlin and in my ignorance I traveled this country without the mandatory East German Visa.

The four of us from the freighter now sat in one coupé for the remainder of the rail journey to Berlin. Wound up, I was eager to talk and spill my story of my night walk, but I could say nothing that was appropriate without having the conversation skillfully averted. I was discreetly kicked in the chins or painfully pinched in the waist. Who were all those strangers?

It was barely daylight when we pulled into the East Berlin station. By now I knew the West station was my destination. The gray lady with the quiet man behind her like a shadow departed. Through the coupé window, the middle aged woman and I witnessed a welcoming committee of formally uniformed East German Government officials, bowing respectfully to the old gray lady, as she was escorted in their midst, the quiet man following by a respectful distance.

The middle aged woman with a big sigh of relief finally strongly reprimanded me. "Traveling without visa and a big talker, I almost lost you." She explained she often took this passage from Denmark, through East Germany, because it was the shortest even though more dangerous route to Berlin. She had previously met the gray lady, always escorted, and she expected her to be a powerful East German party member. I could have easily been imprisoned in this undemocratic sliver of backcountry. Indeed this lady had been my guardian angel. Our next stop after the inspection was West Berlin and Friedriechstrasse station. We parted with warm hugs, and she couldn't resist some friendly advice.

This early morning I arrived at family Reich's to their great surprise. Traveling all night and with the earlier events still vivid,

I was too wound up for sleep. I set out for the recommended job interview, but I eventually was hired by another fashion house that same day. It was now more complex. As many native Berliners in the fashion field were unemployed, now as an American, a foreigner, I had to prove skills that could not be equaled by a German. The firm's able account manager composed a letter stating that I was hired as an interpreter, fashion designer, pattern maker and designer model. To my surprise patterns were actually made from my figure because I was supposed to have an ideal figure. With all these qualifications, a native could not easily replace me. So now I gained experience in sportswear and in the leather goods market and was able to save up for my forthcoming trip across the continent.

Staying with my relatives, I was offered the living room couch. They were heavy smokers, and we were engulfed in heavy smoke with little ventilation. Yet I was grateful for this shelter and the company. Brigitte, my cousin three years my junior, was happy to have a pal to go out with on the town; dancing is what she loved best. I did not much care about dancing but I complied. So this is how I met Bernd Jochen S. who was to become a good friend and savy local guide.

Young and lithe, I had an abundance of energy and lost no time in signing up for sculpture at the *Hochschule für Bildende Künste* to study with the renowned sculptor, Professor Karl Bobek. I loved the aura of working in the sculpture studio, the excitement of creating a portrait and torsos in clay, working from models. I, the foreigner, received preferential treatment, allowing me extra studio time. This worked to my benefit, as I wanted as little as possible to impose on my relatives. The sculpture I created eventually went on a tour of Europe with Bobek, simultaneously as I traveled the continent.

So Jochen introduced me to Berlin as we traveled about in his old DKW, which broke down frequently but he knew how to fix it. His father and older brother were judges, and he was preparing for this profession too with private tutoring. I learned that this differed in the United States as a judge is appointed, not educated or trained. He would row me in a small boat for hours on the scenic lakes, not trespassing the East - West borders, or we went to hear concerts or opera in East Berlin where the exchange rate was more favorable. He invited me as his date to the annual ball of some elite student fencing club. Men wore tuxedos and he asked me to wear a white gown. Since I was saving money for the Europe trip and had some off - white shantung, I made a gown, fully lined, which met with his approval.

June 20th was my birthday. Jochen surprised me after work, as he had the habit of doing sometimes. I was shocked, the top of his head was bandaged up and with a twinkle of his true blue eyes and his usual charming smile he explained. At the ball another student had asked me for a dance, which I didn't think a serious matter. Being offended Jochen demanded to fight a duel. The opponent's sword edge cut Jochen across the forehead and into the hairline. Being a fine talker and an aspiring future judge, I thought he'd resolve a dispute verbally. I strongly felt that he looked for an occasion to prove the prestigious scar to be dating from his student days. So men had fought a duel over me. I had to chuckle.

My relatives had not mentioned doing anything special for my birthday and Jochen had come to take me out to dinner all tied up in bandages. Of course we went to East Berlin for the favorable rates of exchange. Jochen had picked a fine restaurant by East Berlin standards, and we spent a lovely evening with a glass of wine and a gypsy violinist serenading me. Jochen's charm could make one forget the world's troubles. Now his forehead wrinkled in worries though. He couldn't find enough East or West marks to pay for the dinner. Of course I would help. This was just before pay day, so I had only a small amount to offer. Not expecting this outing, I didn't have my American passport with me. First problems first. He suggested that I head for the bathroom and then discretely leave the restaurant to meet him at the DKW. At an opportune time he would also disappear and meet up with me. Meeting later at the car, we lost no time in disappearing quickly. Behind the wheel his blue eyes met mine and with a most charming smile he offered a plan on how to take me past the border patrol back to West Berlin without a passport.

I didn't agree with his plan but I did not have a choice it seemed. Blossoming with youth and in love, I felt life was exciting, and I planned on making my Europe stay memorable. Many Westerners spent time behind bars in East Germany for small digressions. I also knew one could get shot. After a passionate kiss and a tight embrace I stepped out of that secure old car. Alone, Jochen proceeded towards the Brandenburg Thor and to the strict and inquisitive East German border Schupo control.

It had turned dark now and the large empty field I was now entering was sparsely lit by moonlight, a gray void, adjacent to the inspection station. I wore heels, quietly working myself over the mortar and brick debris remnants of bombed out buildings. My whole concentration was geared to expediently and quietly cover the grounds, trying not to sound the faintest footstep. Step by step I set forth cautiously. My fear was consumed by not being detected by the border police. I was aware that I was trespassing a field of live mines. Daily we were informed in the papers of incidents of *Flüchtlinge,* fugitives trying to escape, meeting death by bullets of the border police or being blown up by mines in the numerous border fields to discourage flight to freedom. The very young or the professionals deserted, those most needed in the faltering communist regime. So as I eased myself across this uneven precipice, I died a hundred deaths. Gently forging each step, I expected an explosion of iron scrap metal to tear into me, rip me apart - just another casualty.

Totally absorbed in my nightmare passage, groping West, Jochen kept an eye on my progress. Just at the appropriate time he proceeded towards the inspection station. With his immense radiant charm and a bandaged head, he was capably able to totally engage the border patrol with his amusing anecdotes. Observing my clearing the field, with jovial departure of the Brandenburg Thor and the much feared police, leisurely he drove on to meet up with me. I think neither one of us would want to repeat our adventure that night. It was the night of my twenty-first birthday.

My relatives had a *Schrebergarten*, a small parcel of land cultivated with fruit trees, a vegetable garden and a splash of flowers for each season. There was a small building but we mostly sat under a shade tree to enjoy lunch or supper set on a table with colorful tablecloth and joined by friends and neighbors. City dwellers often had a country retreat, and this one turned out to be adjacent to the East - West border. A mere barbed wire fence was installed. I could have scaled it if I needed to. Friendly border police would patrol in twos or threes periodically. Greetings would be exchanged; it was a way of life.

My stay was coming to an end as I had set a date on touring the continent. My relatives were strongly opposed to my continuing on this trip, claiming that I was much too thin and frail for such an ordeal. Considering themselves guardians on my mother's behalf, they insisted on my having a medical check up with their doctor. I felt energetic but I thought best to abide by their demands. The doctor's verdict was that indeed I was well and healthy but he too suggested I forego such an exhausting months long trip. I was not as heavy boned and strong with lower body weight as the average German. Nevertheless being of legal age now, I thought it was my decision.

There were border disputes and political turmoil to be concerned about and even the eventuality of war. Jochen informed me that his age group would be the first to be enlisted into the military in case of war. He would fight for his *Vaterland*, if he must, but his free spirit wanted to enjoy a more casual life. He too was concerned about my leaving Berlin and that we would never to meet again, as I eventually must depart for America. In his convincing manner he tried to assure me that "marriage was no cemetery of youth."

Time was short, and we both felt the pain but did not talk about the parting. We lived as if there were no tomorrow. One night, Jochen unexpectedly drove his often-ailing DKW out into the lake area. He was a native and knew the Berlin countryside well with all its complex and obscure borderlines. I fully trusted him. On this moonlit summer night he parked under the majestic oaks as we dipped bare into the pleasantly mild warm lake. Not having planned this outing, we didn't bring bathing suits. We frolicked about making waves, which reflected rippled moons light. It was a beautiful night, a moment not to be repeated. Then, free of any care, we ran and played trying to dry off. In that spacious DKW, bedded on old blankets we made passionate love for the last time. Oblivious of the world, we existed just for one another, wanting these moments to last an eternity.

Jochen's head lifted in attention to a faint outside signal. The magic spell broken, I too followed his gaze. Our nude bodies entwined, we observed, faces pressed against the vehicle windows, all around us. Uniformed border police on night duty totally surrounded us. In utter disbelief no one spoke a word. Jochen rose gently, gallantly facing the multitude. He grasped their attention only as he could with that magnetic charm, more so as our lives depended on it. Recalling scenes of the famous spy Mata Hari, she worked in the nude, nights, and when surprised, seduced any predator. Experienced in the modeling circuit, I only needed a fraction of a moment to get into some clothing. Beyond the initial surprise, some hard questioning and answering lasted most of the night. Eloquently Jochen insisted on having missed a turn in the dark on an unfamiliar road. Jochen's charm won after hours of interrogation with an icy warning that a subsequent meeting on East German land would put us behind bars.

Seven years later we met again in southern Germany when I had returned from a trip behind the Iron Curtain. Jochen was now a full-fledged judge at the Wimar court. Neither one of us had forgotten that night. We shared those times just before the wall was erected to divide the two sectors of Berlin.

15 Experiencing the European Continent d

AT THE ANTWERP train station *Tante* Lenchen, my grandmother's niece and *Onkel* Franz her husband, received me with a warm welcome. I was taken to a party where only Flemish was spoken, but my relatives spoke German and French as well. The next morning we viewed their house under construction, a magnificent villa and their pride. It had just been sanctioned, a custom when the roof outline is scaled in, a small pine tree was erected on the uppermost structure of the still incomplete building for blessings with a beer bash for the workers.

Also here in Antwerp on the first of July 1961, I met with my Australian friends Bill and Frank to commence our 11,400 - mile journey of the European continent with an antique automobile that had failed the ten-year road test in England. Bill, an engineer was mechanically inclined and was to keep a close watch on the vehicle. He then informed me that he had gotten engaged to an Australian girl in London and as we were traveling in a group for economics, he offered to portray the big brother. He thought that would give him ample opportunities to lecture me for the next three months.

None of us could have taken this trip on our own. So on this first night camping I quickly learned to give up comfort and cleanliness to first establish companionship. The guys slept in one tent and I occupied the other. We each had chores. Bill and Frank, also an engineer, shared the driving as well as the loading and unloading of supplies each night and setting up the tents. Bill also expediently looked after the vehicle, named Lolita. On a little camp stove I prepared the evening meals. The guys only spoke Australian English, so for the duration of the trip, as if connected by an umbilical cord I did whatever translating. Starting out with travel brochures in various languages, I planned the trip, the sights we'd do in each town, of course choosing my preferences like museums and the art scenes. Frequently we took guided tours as our stay in each town was brief. I quietly translated for the guys word for word and often other tourists joined in a circle for the translation as well.

We traveled the Netherlands. The biggest village was Den Haag, Madurodam, a miniature village we saw in the pouring rain, and then with joyful venture explored canals of the new and old Amsterdam. In my former home town Hamburg we enjoyed a boat trip on the Binnenalster, one of the beautiful lakes primarily used for sailing within this metropolis. At night we viewed the harbor with its ocean liners, freighters and barges and then had a

On 3 months tent camping tour throughout
Europe with Australians Bill Farrar,
Frank McGuire, Bob Brownfield, 1961

157

drink at the Reperbahn, one of those well known bars frequented by sailors. We also traveled on picturesque back roads passing straw thatched farmhouses and went on to wonderful, wonderful Copenhagen. We rented bikes to acquaint ourselves with this town. Much of the busy traffic consisted of bikers taking separate bike trails and following strict traffic rules. Of course we paid a visit to the much admired and charming mermaid resting on a rock close to shore. Tivoli garden, the unique amusement center, was a delightful repose. This was followed by a stormy wet night in our tents.

Lolita was lodged onto a freighter crossing the Strait of the North Sea to Sweden. On our way to Stockholm we saw houses laying low, their roofs covered with grass and flowers. Arriving late at the camp ground, we groped our way into some empty spots. We experienced thunderous heavy rains that night, and accumulated rivulets of water ran down to the low areas. Waterlogged and drenched, we had to abandon our tents, as we nearly drowned. We spent precious time drying out clothing and sleeping bags. I've learned that we took showers whenever they were offered, mostly of cold water. These shower stalls were separate for the genders but open to the viewing public. Scandinavians were not as inhibited. On cobblestones we toured Stockholm admiring the heavy, simple Nordic architecture. Passing picturesque lakes we found ourselves in Oslo and enjoyed our first hot shower since camping out. Frognerparken offered a magnificent sculpture garden, *kon tiki* Viking Museum and last the biggest Olympic ski jump, Holmenkollen. Bergen, on the Norwegian Sea, was a little jewel of town, the dearest to me, embedded around fjords and snow covered mountains.

I stepped unfortunately into a wasps nest and then tried to soothe the pain by dipping into an icy cool lake. At the camp ground we met a group of New Zealanders and Aussies. Keeping warm with hot coffee, we talked late into the cold rainy night. On a boat trip we viewed a magnificent sunrise above the fjords, this being our last joint outing with Frank. He had to return to London, and Bob was to join us in Köln to continue a threesome for the remainder of the trip. Meanwhile the *Kronen* were just running through our fingers.

Time was approaching for us to connect with Bob, and it turned out to be a wild race. We missed the ferry to Denmark. We again missed the second ferry but with luck from Göteburg, ours was the last car to embark. Getting little rest, Bill made haste through Denmark. We slept brief periods in the car, had a chance for an ice cold shower on the way, and passing Hamburg made it in time. Even on a tight schedule, we knew it was a luxury, but we allowed a full day of rest in Köln.

Again we were a threesome now with Bob C. a business man who talked much about his wonderful secretary who became Miss Australia. We toured the Bundestag in Bonn, with an informative lecture offered. On with our whirlwind tour to idyllic - romantic Heidelberg on the Neckar. In the cool evenings we now accustomed ourselves taking walks at leisure, viewing the University and castle. In Stuttgart we saw the Schillerplatz and yet another castle. We traveled on to the luscious green valleys and hills of Switzerland, dotted with cows, and on to Zurich where we camped near a lake. Such close togetherness at times just got me mad at my men and I sneaked off to be alone and went swimming. There always seemed to be an immediate search party for me and freedom was short lived. We snacked on wonderful Swiss chocolate and cheese to our hearts content. In the high country, we traveled fertile valleys surrounded by snow covered mountains, listening to the ever reverberating echoes of cow bells. In Bern on the river Aare we viewed the parliament and cathedral. Our coldest night was in Grindelwald, camping in the snowy valley near Alpenhorn in magnificent sight of the Jungfrau and glaciers stretching out far. The principality of Lichtenstein had the castle its main attraction. In Austria we admired blue-green lakes on mountain drops with its magnificent ornate Schloss Linderhof, as in Oberammergau, then in contrast the sparse monastery. In Munich, more formal, I wore a dress to take in the town. With former Traphagen classmate Ele we enjoyed a merry chat at the *Hoffbräuhaus*. If there had been space in our cramped quarters she would have been game to join us. Heilbrunn - Schloss in Salzberg, was where we viewed the salt mine with its underground tunnels, riding rails. I was admired for my quick and accurate translations. The first and only night away from the guys due to heavy rains was spent in a youth hostile. Then in Vienna we enjoyed a beautiful and restful campsite in the high country. Viewing the impressive parliament with sculptures of justice and fairness, and so along the beautiful blue Danube we headed for Italy.

This then was my introduction to tropical southern Europe. In Venice, with bleached dwellings, paint peeling, webbed narrow canals, commuting is done by gondolas or water busses and beyond view of the beautiful Adriatic Sea. We shopped at the colorful markets, walked the *Ponti di Realto* bridge, took in the Grand Canal, St. Marco Palace, the magnificent Plaza. As a special treat we saw the highly accomplished Italian art of glass blowing. Below sea level, and noticeably damp, we camped the night tortured by rats. In the art city, Florence, in great heat we visited the Dom - Cathedral where we admired Michelangelo's works. Old Masters were represented in *Pligli Uffizi Galbrie*. Then an overall view over town, all red tile roofs from *Pizziale*

Michelangelo high point. This was my first exposure to great heat and I nearly passed out. In cooler night, violins sounded passionate tunes as we acquainted ourselves with the town. Yes, now wonderful Rome with abundant sculptures and fountains, more of Raphael and Michelangelo frescos in the Vatican and St. Peter's Basilica.

The guys had taken a meal that didn't agree with them, and after mothering them for a day I then ventured off alone. With difficulty I found my way in the old narrow streets. Persistently the fiery race of Latinos troubled me wherever I turned. Roman ruins, Forum and Coliseum were at length explored and admired.

I also managed an interview with Señor Rapuano of a world renown fashion house. He showed impatience as we had difficulty conversing, and I decided I didn't desire to work there and yet try to learn another language. With blistering feet I walked the *Via Veneto*, refreshed my bare feet in the *Font di Trevi* fountain. I walked on to the Olympia Stadium of 100,000 seats and enjoyed many more grand sculptures. At Anzio, we camped on the beaches of a beautiful coast and again I looked for solitude from the guys. I met a young Italian journalist, conversing in French about our differing cultures. Meanwhile the guys had been frantically looking for me again and wasted no time notifying the police about my disappearance, after handing them my passport. Late at night after strong reprimands we consoled.

At Napoli on the Tyrrhenian Seas, we saw slums and much poverty, children begging, being caught at taking Bill's wallet out of his pocket. We met Bill's parents, on world tour by boat and we elegantly dined aboard their ship. With these lovely people we toured Pompeii, Palermo and Capri where oranges, lemons and figs grew in profusion.

On our own again we visited the leaning tower of Piza,

climbing the narrow leaning stairs and then grateful to have made it back to the ground again. At various locations during our trip we retrieved our mail at an American Express office. In Milan I heard worrisome news of Berlin. East West conflict over the Berlin issue made headlines. Communists were about to isolate and starve the free city of Berlin, have it collapse and surrender. I was concerned for the city having experienced narrow survival firsthand, the welfare of my relatives and not least my possessions of wardrobe trunk and luggage - all I owned.

Despite stony beaches the Italian Riviera was lovely on the azure blue Mediterranean Sea with subtropical plants in abundance and with stately palm trees. I received strong admonitions about swimming from the guys but nevertheless enjoyed getting to know the coastal towns by swimming nearly its length. Much anticipated Monaco radiated its beauty, wealth and a harbor of magnificent yachts. In contrast the camp ground was dirty with no washing facility and odors of toilets and disposal. Despite odds I managed to dress up for a night at the well known Monte Carlo Casino. My translating attracted some Americans who asked for my help. So to this group I explained the rules and interpreted for their gambling. A tour of the princely palace and splendor of Prince Albert and American born Princess Grace was a joy.

Back in France, in Nice I swam two hours along the coast, covering sights of the town. That same evening we walked the beach for 7 - 8 miles and then did more walking in town. The Russian Orthodox church dating from 1912 had colorful ornate decorations and portraits imbued with pearls. Cannes is known for its international film festival and was a destination for the jet set. Here again I did seek refuge at sea with a coastal swim trying to calm myself about troubles in Berlin, which now was developing into a crisis.

At Marseilles we took a boat ride to the *Chateau Dill*, where the Count de Monte Christi was imprisoned. We toured the island and fortress, all very bare. Avignon, Pont du Gard, offered an old Roman bridge. Along the French Riviera we crossed the Pyrénées, our last leg of the journey to Spain, the Costa Brava on treacherous roads and stormy weather but with exquisite panorama of the sea. I explored the beautiful bay, took a long swim, went snorkeling and climbed cliffs, giving thanks to the Lord for this sojourn. The guys were concerned about my staying out too long as they did not enjoy swimming. Because the many hours we spent driving I needed exercise and the extra bath.

Barcelona was my first and only experience of a bullfight. I delighted in the matador's dance and the richly decorated and colorful robes and was able to capture some quick sketches for future reference. Six steers were killed on a lame and blind horse. This I did not care for, gruesome.

On a lighter side that night we enjoyed flamenco dancing and fireworks to musical waterworks in front of the National Gallery. I remembered Valencia for us being totally waterlogged in another stormy night. The sea looked like gray - green foamy waves, it was a grueling night. Lolita got stuck in the desolate desert south of town when an English group came for rescue. We passed poor villages on bumpy and broken streets. We found many Catholic churches resplendent in art but the people were poor, garbed in black, ancient appearing ladies bent over with steep hunches, frail and tiny. Many lived in mountain caves or mere holes. Granada, situated in mountainous land, also meant Moorish Castle.

Gibraltar, once a Moorish stronghold, became the British rocky fortress, where the saying goes, "As long as the wild monkeys inhabit these rocks, British rule will persist." Monkeys were abundant, harmless and had free rein. One was warned that they may take off with unattended purses. We delighted in their games. In heat and exhaustion we were now down to one meal per day. This international duty free port attracted many bargain hunters.

We sailed the Strait of Gibraltar for Tangiers, Morocco with magnificent views of the heavily inhabited rocky fortress. This proved the high point of our unusual exotic venture. When we arrived, Hassan, our charming guide forced himself upon us, convincing us he was the best. We followed him through narrow passages of Jewish and Arabic quarters, bizarre market places with ragged shapeless figures. Veiled women and men appraised us tourists with dark faces and inquisitive eyes. Hassan protected me from their advances. At the bazaar we become entranced with a snake charmer, as he enticed with flute and drums a giant snake out of a woven basket. Tourists abound with cameras as the charmer pulls me into the center, Bill grabs my camera. In a trance to the exotic tune, this giant reptile very slowly encircles me as our guide stands motionless and my companions seem only interested in capturing this phenomena on film. Hypnotized, incapable of fear and movement, I stand encircled by the rhythmic motion of the snake tightening its embrace, all this taking an eternity of time. Later more relaxed we took hot mint tea at a café of Hassan's choice. In the cool evening we whiled away on the beautiful beach with the purest white sand.

In Seville, during days of brutal heat we learned to take pleasant evening strolls to admire the Moorish influenced architecture. We viewed lovely back scene terraces, palm gardens and experienced unquenchable thirst. Again I longed for some solitude from my grumbling companions. At the campground we met a group of German tourists and discussed the Berlin situation, leaving me highly concerned as I figured that I may not be able to return. No word from my relatives.

Entering scenic Portugal we stopped in a small town to change currency in a bank. Our international group attracted major attention, with the bank director personally attending and advising me. My profession stated on my passport, fashion designer from New York, Berlin, stirred excitement and invited many questions. We toured through *Lisbon* in the cool of night, and we loved the view of town from the old fortress. I couldn't get accustomed to men's starring eyes. Over beer and olives with our guide we discussed politics late into the night. It proved a challenge, in limited Spanish and French to converse about the situation of Angola then in Portuguese administration versus Berlin, rule divided by four world powers and threatened by communism.

In Nazaré a Portuguese traditional coastal fishing village, we encountered fishermen in wide black pump pants, checkered shirts, long black peaked hats, cumberbunds and barefooted. We saw ancient appearing women, young girls and children in wide checkered or dark skirts with many white petticoats, covered with large scarves. Heads and faces were half hidden from the sun, everyone was barefoot. In the background raged the blue green surf in morning mist. Life here is partaken at the beach. The women were on knees, cleaning fish, and men repairing nets. In a small coastal restaurant we enjoyed a wonderful several course seafood dinner. Entry at the sanctuary of Fatima was denied to us for lack of wearing long pants and my not being covered with a headdress.

My interpreting was challenged particularly one night by a Spanish policeman stopping us for a burned out rear light bulb. What I lacked in language skills I had to compensate for in charm or playing naïve. Good naturedly we ended up giving the police officer a lift to Toledo with lively discourse during the trip. Now at the Prado Museum a treat of El Greco, Velazquez, Goya, Michelangelo with representation of Italian and German masters. I toured the Prado with a pleasant and knowledgeable Spaniard, but again had to decline a date as my guys wouldn't have approved. On to *Palacio Real* castle, acclaimed one of the most beautiful and richest in cultural collections of Europe.

We crossed the Pyrénées back into France, San Sebastián being the last stop of our journey in Spain. We toured the Bordeaux wineries, vineyards, cellars and amply tasted their fine products. At Châteaux La Tour Hout Brion, the owner himself took us on tour. Men in high boots trampled the grapes in a large wooden bay. Grapes were separated from the stems and each, grapes and stems crushed, then juice of each mixed together in a wooden barrel kept to rest for 3 - 4 weeks. For the remainder of the fermenting they were put in small wooden barrels for at least one year in cellars kept at 13 - 17 degrees Celsius, and bottled after this stage. Majestic vineyards spread as far as the eye could scan with small groups of pickers at harvest. I did not feel well. Was it the unaccustomed wine sampling or our soon to be parting in Paris?

Our last joint camp site was in the Bois de Boulogna, Paris, taking a modest meal as we rested up. In major cities we collected our mail at American Express. I also made inquiries at *Gare du Nord* for my train ride to Berlin to retrieve my belongings. Soon to be on my own, I told myself, "be smart - keep a clear head." After three months of togetherness, a generous parting gift from Bill's parents was an evening out in Paris. Again I followed my own advice, to enjoy life and each minute of pleasurable circumstances as I can, no telling what the morrow may bring. The three of us in wrinkled clothes, elegantly dined at Aux Mervelles des Mers. The program at the *Moulin Rouge* was from 11 PM until 3 AM. We consumed a couple of bottles of champagne, delighted in the famous Can Can Girls raving costumes and their performances, half dressed women with beautifully shaped legs. From this 'dream' we headed for our damp tents for what remainder of our last night. In the morning we visited the Louvre, and then the guys were helpful in finding me accommodations. At the Hôtel de L'Etoile d'Or, I had my first hot bath in three months and the guys cleaned up as well. After a last meal, we had a painful farewell at the American Embassy. Embraces, kisses - farewell my brothers.

15 Experiencing the European Continent e

Paris II

WHEN I RETURNED to Paris at the end of my European travels, I immediately signed up at the *Alliance Française* to further improve my French. At the German Consulate I was assured that travel to Berlin was still possible despite increased East - West tensions and border restrictions. I missed connections with friend Jochen in Paris as planned. He fell asleep behind the wheel from Germany and crashed his DKW but was not hurt. An interview at the de Ricci's in Avenue Matignon assured me of a position as live-in *jeune fille*, teaching English to three young children. I connected with pal Chantal Dumont who promptly invited me to a much famed show at high style fashion house Balenciaga. She now again resumed modeling, between more facial surgeries due to her automobile accident. Finally I then took the train to West Berlin to pick up my belongings, all I owned. The city was now completely sealed off and once again I surprised my relatives. Yes, I survived the Continental trip they feared I was too frail to partake in, and I even fared well. Once again we had coffee at the *Laube* in their *Schrebergarten* with uniformed armed guards patrolling at the wire fence. There were great sorrows as families in East Berlin and the East sector could no longer extend visits. It was August 13, 1961, when the Berlin Wall was errected, with many future lives to be lost in desperate crossings to freedom. Brigitte had left home and caused her parents great anguish. The political outlook was grim with the only hope of the United States coming for rescue. The following day the Reich's took me plus wardrobe trunk and ample luggage to West Berlin rail station, which was still in service.

That very night in Paris, I dined with my new host family in the kitchen over pleasant conversation for the first and only time in English. Coincidentally, Madame de Ricci's father, a general, had been in charge over the French sector of Berlin after WWII. Monsieur de Ricci practiced international law, was a judge and worked out of a suite in the apartment. Both spoke German and English but after this evening for the remainder of my stay we only conversed in French with my doing an occasional German - English translation for Monsieur. They lived off *Champs Illysee*, past *Le Figaro* newspaper and the whole block belonged to the grandparents. The Count and Countess de Ricci lived on the ground floor. A winding white marble staircase lead to the top floor apartment. Florence age nine, Sophie age seven and Nicholas age four were my charges to look after and to teach English. This left me time for my studies, and so for the time I was taken care off.

Mornings I tended the children, breakfasted and took them to school, myself attending the *Alliance Français,* and then I would retrieve them at noon. We had our main meal with the parents at noon in the dining room. Ellen, the cook, served us. After lunch we took coffee in the formal living quarters where we relaxed, Monsieurs only time of day to enjoy the children. The children let loose. Monsieur apologized for not ever reprimanding them, time with their children was so sparse. I had an hour to myself, and then we spent time in the park. The de Ricci's were very pleasant, and I worked hard to improve my language skills. The children cried a lot and quarreled much with one another and cost patience but they had become dear to me. Initially the children were critical of my speech, especially my grammar, but with time my French improved to their approval.

The children had gone to sleep, and we expected four dinner guests. In my position I was expected to partake in the formalities. It was a formal dinner with the finest assortment of French wines offered and with Ellen the cook serving. Sadly, on these occasions my language proficiency was far lacking but still by osmosis I benefited. Yet I had come to Europe to acquire knowledge, grow more mature, and with an older face, I hoped to succeed in the fashion world in the States. I felt right on course.

My travel companions Bill, Frank and Bob with a group of other Aussies from London, were now planning a van trip through Europe, Near East, Far East and back to Australia, completing their world tour. Bill called off his engagement to the Australian girl, so he was now in hot pursuit to marry me and bring me to Australia within a few months. I enjoyed hearing about their adventures of sparsely traveled roads in far off exotic lands. Yet Bill could not understand that I could not readily accept his proposal and give up what I had so diligently worked and fought for.

In my free time I pursued the Parisian art scene, taking in the new exhibits at the Louvre, the Tuilleries, Musée Art Moderne, galleries, Quartier Latin, Sacre Cour, theatre and opera. All my connections were French or French speaking. Yet I felt I achieved little. Perhaps there is a dead point in everyone's life. The family had gone off to Courjanvier in Montorgis, the Count's estate. I lunched with Monsieur, the Viscount, attended by Ellen, and was informed that he had received his doctorate in Spain and was disclosing about his interesting international case works. On some other occasions, the children and I lunched with the grandparents, the Count and Countess de Ricci on the ground floor

apartment in a much more formal setting attended by the butler Q. The Countess had a personal handmaid, and I wondered
how she kept busy. The Count was Director of the Louvre and
indeed I was awed by the fine art collection displayed in the dining room, living quarters and library. During our conversation I
was discretely warned of Arab predators, abducting young blond
women for their Near East harems. In Paris supposedly many
young fair maidens had permanently disappeared.

Algeria was seeking independence from France between
1961 - 62. This prompted what was known as the Algerian re-
volts. During my stay we were exposed to fierce bombings and
explosions of important government and civil buildings as well
as automobiles in every quarter in Paris. We were on curfew during late evening hours. In the middle of one night an explosion
seemed very close. Literally I fell out of bed as I gathered the
frightened children. The morning news brought us the devastation of the previous night. It happened in our very own building,
consisting of a block, starting at the Champs Ellyssee where *Le
Figaro,* the daily newspaper operated and proudly displayed its
sign. An explosion had ripped apart the facing and interior of the
business. I had left perilous Berlin and now faced more anguish.

There were hunting parties at the estate, and we all took the
two-hour long car ride to participate in the festivities following
the hunt. The children and I enjoyed long walks in the woods
and pastures where sometimes we collected mushrooms in small
baskets. On occasion the children and I spent time at Courjanvier
alone, only the pleasant butler Q. and a cook attending. In my
tender youth, I missed Paris and felt here like "bird in a golden
cage."At the dinner gatherings, in time I felt more at ease as my
language skills improved, slowly opening the door of knowledge
and understanding.

THE IMMIGRANT

Of my former Jacques Heim studio friends, Mademoiselle Lenoir the French seamstress, Rudolph the Austrian tailor and Jacques the designer, had a parting rendezvous, the occasion of Jacque's return to Holland. I kept in touch with the fashion world and worked up an elegant wardrobe for myself. I welcomed every invitation to fashion shows. My American passport stated my profession as fashion illustrator - designer and some fashion houses denied me access to their shows. Chez Dior was one of them. Rudolph was working there now and had obtained me a privileged invitation. It was my top priority to attend. At the Alliance Française I had met a Yugoslav architect, his wife a medical doctor was visiting. So with the help of her Yugoslav medical doctor's passport, investing in a black fur hat, to hide my blonde mane, changing my identity to a brunette, I passed inspection. It turned out to be the most exquisite show I ever attended, witnessing the prettiest, most feminine and elegant gowns. Meanwhile I fiercely perspired under the black fur hat, acquired just for this occasion, in a well heated salon and of fear for someone to faint and call for the doctor present. That night with photographic memory I sketched the complete collection.

Christmas was spent at Courjanvier with family and guests. They insisted I should not spend the holiday alone in Paris, so in a separate car with the count and countess, myself in the back seat with the hounds, we proceeded to the estate. During this trip English was spoken for my comfort. It was a beautiful life and being waited on by servants and butler agreed with me, but the same, I missed my freedom. I was given the lovely guest room never occupied by *jeune fille's*. Christmas morning, early, the children excitedly joined me in bed. Later, all in bathrobes, gifts were exchanged. I was touched to receive from the countess a blue leather bow napkin ring, only reserved for immediate family. I felt accepted and it was hinted at of finding me a suitor in their clan. We feasted on turkey and enjoyed choice wines and Champagne dated 1929.

New Years holiday with Chantal, her boyfriend Michael and mannequin friend Taxi, we departed for Grenoble to ski the French Alps. Michael's parents owned large food processing concerns and lived in the mountains. New Year's Eve we partook in a well attended party with night long celebration. There was beautiful powder snow and I learned to love to ski.

I had to obtain a visa extension to remain in France, and *Monsieur* offered to take care of this little matter as he had connections. But on my day off instead, I stood in a long line at the *Prefecture de Police* to get my extension. During this long wait in line, I became acquainted with Dr. Salman Kataye also seeking an extension. He was Syrian and had formerly obtained his doctorate at the Sorbonne. With a busy day practice in his own country, he also spent too many nights delivering babies, claiming that he didn't get enough rest. Now he was studying to specialize and then return to his home.

With Salman I shared a passion for art. We enjoyed much time together during the remainder of our stays until summer in the Louvre, the Quartier Latin, the Rodin Museum, Sacre Cour and galleries about town. He introduced me to the haunting French poem "Barbara" and the process of etching, done in his small room beneath the roof, one of those well romanticized attic dwellings. It was a happy time but we both felt a need to return to our own countries, to work from the foundation of knowledge we each had acquired. Salman felt indebted to help his people in Syria. He could not fathom me draped in veils without opportunity to exercise freedom and creativity. Parting is always painful, a process of priorities and decision making. We give up something and hope to attain what we estimate is right for us spiritually.

Parting with the de Ricci's was strained, as they had wanted me to stay on longer and in exchange given me the use of the apartment for the summer. My urgent return, I stated, was getting a fashion job in New York before the slow summer season and my concern for income after a two-year absence in Europe. May 31, 1962, Salman took me to the *Gare du Nord* for the train to Le Havre to embark on the *MS Aurelia*. His previous melancholy stemmed from the fact that neither of us could alter the course.

On our Atlantic crossing, a few days of rough sea got our international student group seasick on this small Italian freighter. Belatedly we arrived in New York City June 8th where on dock I was greeted by Judith and Mike S., whose West side apartment I was to occupy while he conducted his summer orchestra in Aspen, Colorado. That night we toasted with Champagne at Stuart's in lively discussions, with Judith's plans for a journey to Greece emerging. During the summer my foremost responsibility was to keep Stuart's prize antique musical instrument, his base, well humidified.

16 Settling Down

AFTER A TWO-YEAR separation from my family, first off, I went for a visit to Toronto. My sister had just departed for Germany for a prolonged stay. My mother had gotten married to Bruno Loeffler, a very likable widower and fellow immigrant, and they were now living in Thornbury, Ontario on the Georgian Bay. He had a nine-year-old son, Bodo. Bruno was totally bald. He had no eyebrows, nor hair on his eyelids or anyplace on his body. Bruno had spent days in a *Bunker*, the building destroyed during an air raid in Berlin. The shock of being isolated and with help slow to excavate the survivors, this experience instantly cost him loosing all his hair. With humor and a positive disposition he gave a handsome appearance. I was to visit this very northern Canadian town often, if only to fortify myself in good company. Rollie Zavada came to visit me here. Our friendship kindled at about my just having

With sister Elfi and Senta, 1965

completed high school. I had received some art recognition and consequently invited to Rochester University for a social function. Rollie attended there part-time for his masters degree and so we met there at the dance floor. We dated infrequently in Rochester and then New York. Now again we connected after my two-year European stay. Here now we hiked for hours along the frigid waters of the aqua colored Bay, considered one of the purest large bodies of water in the northern hemisphere.

Rollie would land his Cessna 182 on the rural landing strip between Collingwood and Thornbury. Circling low over the remote acreage was his way of alerting us to pick him up by car. He owned a parachute but had not yet had the courage to use it. Would I join him for sky diving lessons and a jump? We made a date. Close to New York in Orange, Massachusetts, we went parachuting, recording the day's event on film. It was an exhilarating experience sailing carefree through the sky, and that night over dinner, Rollie proposed to me. From there on much of our traveling was done in the small Cessna as we then set out next to see his large Czechoslovakian family in Gary, Indiana. During our renewed short courtship he took many flights to New York. We enjoyed Broadway productions and sightseeing the city with its many fine museums and gourmet dining.

I prepared a new portfolio and landed the fashion design job I had left Paris for. I was content in Europe, yet I had missed that special dynamic energy of New York. Now I gave attention to my loungewear design position when unexpectedly early Stuart returned to reclaim his apartment. It was a mad dash to find my own temporary place.

Lee, a Russian Jewish immigrant friend from Traphagen, had meanwhile opened her own boutique. She traded my designs for dresses to prepare a wardrobe for my marriage. Rollie's cousin, a jeweler helped us design the rings and select a diamond. Meanwhile wedding plans were to be held in Thornbury, traditionally with the brides parents. A month long honeymoon continental tour of South America was planned later for February.

Rollie decided as a new citizen that Washington D.C. would be educational. We took in the White House, Lincoln Memorial, Jefferson Memorial, the Capital, Washington Memorial and most beloved to me a glimpse of the Smithsonian. I could have easily spent a whole week in that museum alone. All this we topped off dining at a good German restaurant.

My preparations for the wedding were a simple ankle length gown in poi de soi, headpiece, bracelette and white silk shoes selected at Lord & Taylor's. I trained a new designer to take my position before departing for Rochester. On December 22, 1962, we had an intimate church wedding with only the immediate family. Remote Thornbury was enveloped in deep white snow with subfreezing temperatures.

Challenges for me started at the beginning of the marriage, as Rollie was thirteen years older, and was an accomplished film and television engineer at Eastman Kodak. He enjoyed many hobbies which he expected his young bride to adopt. Immediately after the ceremony we departed in his white Simca sports car, which frequently broke down, for a mini honeymoon to Grey Rocks Inn, St. Jovite in Quebec. This was my formal introduction to a week of ski lessons. I loved to ski and caught on quickly but struggled to keep up with my expertly skiing husband.

I became the all around student. My busy life entailed lessons in driving, skiing, tennis, flying, cooking and formally entertaining. In our one bedroom apartment I hosted our first dinner guests, friends of Rollie, the wife working as a nutritionist at Eastman Kodak. A novice, of course I was nervous entertaining a food expert. In our modest and cramped kitchen I set out our new dishes and silverware with a single candle lighted on a small table. I served simply a beef roast, scalloped potatoes, vegetables and salad with dessert. Everyone ate heartily, the conversation was animated, and I even received compliments.

So convenient to Rollie's work schedule, we now set off for our honeymoon to South America which proved to be a memorable extravagance, a month of touring first class. We started out in the new capital of Brazil, Brazília, then, Belo Horizonte, beautiful coast fronted Rio de Janeiro, São Paulo – Argentina, Buenos Aires, the magnificent Iguaçu falls bordering Brazil, Argentina and Paraguay – the luscious and lovely Chilean coast, Valparaíso and Santiago – Peru, Lima and viewing the ancient Inca ruins of Machu Pichu. A stop at Bogotá, then the impressive Panamá Canal – Mexico City, Acapulco. I did all the translations in Spanish as Rollie did not speak another language. Despite all required inoculations most of the trip I was sick and weakened, but beautiful impressions remain.

Three weeks into the marriage Rollie announced that he had made an appointment for me at Rochester University to have my IQ tested. Claiming to have an IQ of a genius, he expected the mother of his children to be equally intelligent. I felt he should have considered that before our marriage but then he still thought me a perfect match. I refused to be tested and even considered returning to New York. As it later turned out, he proved to have a very low sperm count and could not have children.

I felt it a step down from designing, but I was grateful to find a job as fashion illustrator in B. Forman advertising, the same studio that had given me my first break, now working with a new art director, J. Sondheim. I was again tutored by the senior illustrator and J. Sondheim. Learning at every stage in my new life and expecting to perform expertly started my depressions.

I joined Rollie in many of his business trips of the film and photographic society to Montreal, the west coast and Washington DC. Here first I met Alex Alden, his boss. At the Washington conference he learned of his mother passing away. There had been secrecy of her identity as an influential Russian princess. In later years Alex and I were to become close friends when my path took me to Connecticut.

Although I was admired, even envied for my glamorous job as fashion illustrator, Rollie decided my pay was too low and that it interfered with his taxes. I had to quit. Commitments to various associations, like in his bachelor days kept him occupied nearly every single night and weekends. We saw little of one another except on trips. By now we lived in fashionable Pittsford in an architect designed home. Aside from part-time studies for a degree at Rochester Institute of Technology where I pursued courses in fine art and printmaking, it was not enough of a life for me. He could not perceive that my life was not fulfilled and that I was lonely. I refused to be the maid and hired a housekeeper. It could appear a fairy tale life for the immigrant. I designed my own wardrobe and gowns for the many social functions. Emotionally I could not adjust to the careless riches, not being able to shake my frugal upbringing. The few acquaintances I had proved insincere. Years of poor health and depression in the prime of my life followed. I needed constant doctor appointments. Time passed by without passion. Physical strain and emotional pain proved unbearable. I wanted to resume a life of meaning in New York, but Rollie wouldn't hear of it. I started seeing Dr. Broida, a psychoanalist, which dragged out for years not giving any relief or change.

17 Aviation - Born to Fly a

LIVING IN FASHIONABLE Pittsford, we attended many formal events initiated either by Kodak or Xerox, Rochester's two main employers. I created my own gowns for these functions. I designed them with muslin on a mannequin and sewed them with fabrics carefully chosen from my travels. Also I created a wardrobe for our frequent personal and business trips. Working for a degree in fine arts – printmaking, at Rochester Institute of Technology, entertaining, not least preparing for my pilots license, I was pressed for time. I was the only one in our social group to keep a cleaning lady. This by a young immigrant was an outrage worthy of gossip.

I truly loved to fly. Rollie thoughtfully had taken insurance in case of a flying accident with my mother as the beneficiary. Rollie took his role as flight instructor very seriously. He was a patient teacher and I was his first female student, bragging to his friends how excellent and fearlessly I performed, yet never paying me a single compliment. Whatever I turned to, I was the student with my older and more experienced husband. Mostly I felt discouraged for his holding me off my solo flight.

It was my birthday. I was all dressed up for going out to a fine restaurant, Rollie surprised me by stopping at the airport. He gave me the keys to the Cessna, while he waited in his red Alfa Romero sports car behind the gates. All dressed up, I readied the plane for take off, kicking the tires with my fashionable high heels for proper inflation. After making a roundabout ground flight safety check, I lifted the hood to observe the engine

compartment. Sometimes birds would nest in there near the propeller. A nest with eggs had to be removed. All OK. I swung into
the pilot in command seat. Then ran a flight check following a
chart. All OK. Dialing ground control on one of my three radios,
I was cleared to the active runway. It was a quiet early evening.
No jets waiting in line. Stopping at the prescribed ACTIVE, I
switched to channel 123.5. "Rochester tower, this is Cessna 6284
Alfa - requesting take off." In response, "Rochester Tower, Cessna
6284 Alfa cleared for take off." A last engine check and rev up
of the engine, I turned the plane to either side, as there are no
side view mirrors to possibly detect some unnoticed plane landing. I taxied to the center of the active. Advancing the throttle to
full power and with great acceleration I rolled down the runway.
I loved the ultimate speed and of being in control. The Cessna
begged to be taken off the runway. With sensitive touch I lifted
the plane - it was airborne. Climbing steeply, I next requested
of the tower a right turn out to leave controlled airspace, rather
than a left turn for another go – around or a landing. It was my
solo flight. It was my birthday, and I was going to enjoy it. Free of
another passenger, an instructor and a critiquing husband, joyful
like an eagle I soared the clear blue sky.

My proud instructor husband watched his prize student taking off on her solo flight. Joy turned to horror as I turned away
from the airport, rather, as he had anticipated my immediate return of a go around and to a full stop landing. Not a second lost,
he raced up the flight of stairs to the control tower, two steps at
a time, demanding of the tower operator to order my immediate
return and landing.

Having cleared controlled airspace of the airport, I turned
off the radio. I could not have envisioned a more exciting birthday present as I bounced – glided – soared into a magnificent

sunset. With confidence and skill I performed as I had been taught, getting myself unconsciously farther away from my homeport. Totally enjoying my freedom I now became aware of the setting sun, dusk setting in. I knew the area well as I headed home, it was turning night quickly. We had often flown to Toronto, Quebec, Canada and Gary, Indiana, sometimes at night. Not realizing one had to be checked out for night flying, I performed as I had witnessed and then notified Rochester Tower of my whereabouts and requested landing instructions. Fuming Rollie at their side, calmly the operators gave permission and instructions to land.

17 Aviation - Born to Fly b

Cross Country Flight

I HAD OFTEN been ill and now was waiting for a hospital bed to undergo surgery while Rollie was on a business trip in California. He suggested not wasting time and getting my 200-mile solo cross-country flight out of the way, which kept me from taking my private pilot exam. Not feeling well, but not wanting to be idle, I prepared to take the Cessna 182 to Watertown in northern New York on the St. Lawrence River. This small town near the Canadian border had the highest snow fall recorded in the US, more than Buffalo received, along with some of the fiercest weather conditions.

As a fledgling student pilot, I was aware of the importance of weather, and I made it my business to inform myself to decipher the continuous data spit out of the weather teletype machine. I learned to decode the symbols, and drew myself a weather map, then personally I would speak with the weather adviser. All seemed clear now but a storm was moving in. I was advised to depart as soon as possible to assure a safe return. I followed my flight plan closely, computing time and distances. It was a beautiful clear day as I closely followed the icy emerald colored Lake Ontario coastline. Life was a blast.

I landed in Watertown, taxiing towards the control tower. At the weather station I had my gold embossed logbook initialed for my 200-mile cross country flight and then proceeded computing my return. At that time there were few women pilots, and I became accustomed to glances and special concerns. Weather had deteriorated quicker than expected. While I bent over map and papers, the weather official hovered about me with a serious glance. Airports were still open to VFR flights but on account of impending weather, he advised me to stay the night and if there was an improvement in the morning to proceed my return then. I really did not want to stay the night in that little town. In youthful confidence, surmising the weather picture, I hurriedly completed my flight plan, activated it with the tower personnel and I was on my way.

Having completed about half of my return, clear skies turned overcast and the weather forecast sounded ominous. Cumulonimbus cloud coverings proceeded east towards me at a fast pace with airports starting to close, initially at least to VFR flights. In my young flying experience I had never encountered cumulonimbus conditions, but was advised that such a condition could easily cause wings to be torn off the fuselage. "Best to find yourself on the ground," I counseled myself. It had seemed an easy stretch flying home as I totally concentrated on the radios. This negligence cost me to loose my bearings. I had flown myself off my map. The weather station now reported airports were closing at a steady rate. I did what I had never done before, "I panicked." Truly frightened, I gently pulled the throttle, descending to 500 ft altitude in search of a suitable landing place. I was well experienced in emergency landings, but there just didn't seem a place to set down safely. The highway would have to do. I was aware that I could encounter a fine for landing on a public road or could have my student pilot license revoked, never to fly again. I folded my hands and appealed to our heavenly father. This may have taken just a flash of a moment. I felt calm. Decisively thinking now, hands steady on the controls, I gradually advanced the throttle to regain altitude, foremost in my mind that altitude is safety. With a clear mind I surveyed the terrain 3500 feet below and correctly identified my bearings. Back on the map and on course I headed towards Rochester Municipal Airport. "Rochester tower, this is Cessna 6284 Alfa, on flight plan from Watertown, request landing instructions."The ball was cast in their court whether I could safely land in the storm or not. The guys at Rochester tower, my home port, knew my identity, my ID number of the plane, my voice and once confessed that they never worried about me as they did about some other pilots. Closing my flight plan, I did make the home base before Rochester airport too would close. I had my logbook initialed, having successfully completed my 200-mile cross-country flight. Now I only needed to worry about a vacant hospital bed.

17 Aviation - Born to Fly c

Civil Air Patrol

I HAD NOT been feeling well. When not feeling my sharpest, I wouldn't fly. Nor would I consume alcohol forty-eight hours before anticipated flights, as required. One needed clear senses just to maneuver in controlled airspace of major airports. We had joined Civil Air Patrol. A worthy cause. In their early beginnings pilots volunteered their services, their planes in search and rescue missions. These missions comprised of searching for missing planes, pilots not having closed their flight plans at the end of a journey or were reported overdue on flights by family. My reasons for flying CAP missions were also self-serving. Having a low threshold of pain and should I crash, I wanted someone to come fetch me quickly. I wanted to help my fellow pilots with the hope that someday this would be reciprocated.

A Canadian woman, north of the St. Lawrence River had called in that her husband and two young sons had not returned by night from a flight into the backcountry south of the River. There were no blankets, food or beverages on board. Temperatures in that uninhabited rugged mountainous region were well below zero degrees. A joint Canadian - US mission was organized at daybreak during freezing temperatures that had lingered in the northern hemisphere.

To be fully functioning, we needed a fourth pilot for the all-day mission. Although not well, and against my better judgment, in such a serious case, I offered to make it a foursome. Knowing I would not be feeling better later, I volunteered to fly the first leg. Our group was made up of a Colonel, two Lieutenants, and myself, still a student pilot. Each of us was responsible for our own flight of navigating - fuel - flight plan. As pilot in command I was responsible for the flight, getting us close to the search area, tending radio and instruments while the others were searching for a plane or wreckage.

It was a frosty clear day. I remembered flying other missions. Carl was my flying buddy, he'd gotten his license ahead of me. He loved to fly so much that he'd taken a job at the gas pit, just to be close to planes. When I topped off the Cessna and later the Cherokee, he'd always admonish me to be careful. On a flight plan he was reported missing. We flew the mission and I was shocked to see what a plane looked like, scattered to small pieces all over the landscape. Carl was so young, handsome and full of life's expectations. I cried. Then there was that mysterious mission. A just married young couple, right after the wedding reception departed Rochester Municipal Airport in their Piper Cub. Their honeymoon was to be secret. Parents were alarmed when they did not hear from the couple. Their destination was west, so we flew missions over Lake Erie. With a single engine aircraft one flies at a safe altitude over a large body of water to consider the glide factor to safely return to shore in case of engine failure. We had to fly low to hopefully detect oil slicks on the waves of a downed plane. A long and extensive search found neither their Piper Cub nor the young honeymooners.

My leg ended in Watertown and I moved into the back seat as searcher when another pilot moved into the pilot command seat. All of us except the pilot now were highly concentrating on the frozen, packed snow covered terrain below. We headed for northern New Hampshire, that vast uninhabited wilderness mountain region, south of the Canadian border, where supposedly the father with his two young sons was thought to be missing. At low altitude we combed the virgin snowy white fields, flying over large and small towns, isolated farms, passing ice-covered streams. Then we approached the formidably lonely mountain passes. It took a very experienced pilot at low altitude to safely maneuver our small plane through narrow canyons and closely covering peaks.

Intently, with every fiber of my being, I strained for a visible sign of a crashed plane or sign of cut timber during a possible emergency landing. To be surviving only one night in subfreezing temperatures, ill equipped, possibly injured was itself a miracle. Quietly I wiped away tears so as not to obscure my vision. In this difficult terrain our pilot was taking chances. We all were at risk and we all so desperately wanted to find the survivors and radio for help to the waiting ground crews. Dusk approached and we needed to return with the haunting thoughts of, "if still alive, could they survive another night?"

The Colonel flew the home stretch leg and we were left to our own thoughts and concerns. This was still another mission with a sad ending. Close to our home base, the Colonel informed us that we were out of gas. Most of the day I had valiantly endured abdominal cramps. After a long emotional and exhausting mission I had planned to go to bed as soon as I returned home. Was this yet one more hurdle?

17 Aviation - Born to Fly d

Bermuda Triangle

ROLLIE AND I prepared for a vacation in the Caribbean to escape northern upstate New York's abundant snow and fierce cold, destination Bahamian Islands. We tucked our folding bicycles into the luggage compartment but otherwise traveled light. We then readied the Cessna for our extended cross-country flight. In Washington D. C. we needed to refuel and wanted to stay for the night. It had turned night as we requested landing instructions. It was a super busy commercial airport and one hardly found a chance to speak, as many pilots intended to land and were trying to contact the tower. Worse, sometimes there was static in the reception, and it was difficult to understand the instructions. With three radios it was playing it safe. Due to heavy traffic we were asked to 'hold' over the Pentagon. I'm certain this is no longer permitted after 9/11. It meant flying a tight circle at a low 500 feet altitude until further instructions. It seemed impossible to squeeze in a simple question, "which is the Pentagon?" One lesson flying has taught me, if you need to "make a quick decision and stick with it or take an educated guess," but do something. Inactivity may cost a life.

Even though I was still a student pilot, nevertheless Rollie and I alternated turns, each flying a leg. That meant being responsible for flight planning - acquiring and processing weather information - take offs - piloting in command - landings - refueling. The following day was uneventful as we flew the shortest route with the most favorable winds aloft toward the east Florida coast. It

Self with Cessna 182, destination Bahamas
wearing self inflating life vest

was Rollie's turn to fly the short leg from Fort Lauderdale to West Palm Beach. Cleared for take off, we proceeded down the runway full power for take off. Just before our clearance, windows were closed. Undetected, a bee had gotten into the cockpit. Now as we were rolling down the runway, it now frantically zipped about every direction. Rollie was fatally allergic to bee stings and always carried serum with him. My first thought was that the serum was packed inaccessibly in the baggage compartment. Also, the bee seemed to be more attracted to Rollie as he now started to squirm and madly swung about himself to fend off the elusive bee. I was fully aware of the danger of this distraction during take off. It was noisy in the cockpit, and being soft spoken, I could not easily make myself understood. Whenever I detected some trouble, in bad weather, Rollie needing to tend to the radios or maps, I would gently reach over to his hands on the controls. It was our signal that I was taking over, being accustomed to fly either pilot in command or in the co pilot seat. Rollie tended to the bee while I got us airborne, out of the control zone and to a safe altitude. Windows were opened and with considerable coaxing the bee exited the cockpit.

West Palm Beach was hot and humid. For our destination, West End of Grand Bahamas Islands, Abaco Island, Treasure Cay and Nassau, we needed to cross the Straits of Florida, the shark infested Atlantic. Equipped with a rented self-inflatable raft kept in the back seats and wearing Mae Wests, we filed a flight plan, so if we didn't show up at our destination within a reasonable time, there would be a search. Rollie was in command. It was a relatively short flight, keeping high altitude as safe parameter. We had flown previously over large bodies of water, Lake Erie and Lake Ontario during search and rescue missions, but there weren't any sharks. Rollie did not swim. We kept alert, both of us attentive to the instruments and viewing apprehensively the magnificent aqua colored sea below. When the Bahama Islands came into comfortable landing distance, we started to let down and much of the tension dissipated. We landed at a small landing strip, shed the uncomfortable life jackets, unfolded our bicycles and headed for the remote inn where we had reservations.

A fun-filled carefree week unfolded as we enjoyed isolated white sandy beaches with the purest clear waters to frolic about. On bicycle we ventured into Nassau, sight seeing, shopping the markets and dining at small restaurants offering the tastiest sea-food. Conch and red snapper were my favorites.

Jobs awaited us both, so heavy hearted we proceeded with our return. Via flight plan and again strapping ourselves into our Mae Wests, we departed Nassau airport in pouring rain and heavy fog, IFR [Instrument Flight Regulations] conditions, with Rollie in command. All proceeded well until we got out into the open sea. This was the area called the "Bermuda Triangle" in the Straits of Florida, which we knew nothing about. Just that instant we lost radio communications. All of our three fine radios stayed silent and this under IFR conditions not very distant from any omni, a navigational direction indicator or airport. I was the student as I silently observed Rollie very concerned descending, close to sea level, watching turbulent waves, foaming white heads ever so close beneath us. Rollie had just earned his instrument rating and still lacked experience. It was impregnated in my mind, "altitude is safety." For some unknown fact we both panicked. Never should we have descended so low as to have our fuselage and wings sprayed by the angry tides. At this most precarious situation we barely wrestled the plane off the turbulent, densely fogged sea. Gripped with fear, just silence. It seemed an eternity until Rollie gently lifted the nose of the Cessna to very gradually regain altitude and safety. Now with a safety ledge and clearer thinking, he took a compass heading toward Florida's east coast with still no radio communications until we finally approached Miami.

What had happened? Only much later did I learn about the legends of the Bermuda Triangle. Mysterious disappearances of boats, and all kinds of vessels, later in history airplanes, occurred in this precise triangle without ever communicating their distress. No SOS or MAYDAY signal was ever recorded. For some unknown reason radio communications would break down, as in our experience, and no one ever knew the problems or reasons for vessels vanishing without a trace.

Bone tired we started our home stretch. Rollie insisted he was indispensable at work and planned to arrive on time the next morning. Poor weather persisted with zero visibility. We climbed above the clouds, topping at 16,000 feet to clear blue skies. This was my first experience flying a small unpressurized plane at this high altitude. Gasping for air, we kept a wild conversation going so as not to fall asleep. If I felt this lethargic, we both must have felt the same. I insisted on returning to Miami to wait for more favorable weather.

Late that day we gave it another try. We followed a more favorable weather pattern but it was a longer stretch home. With the day's excitements, we both were tired. Rollie kept drifting off course. Again and again with horror, I noticed the Atlantic below, a full moon reflecting in the glitter of waves. We were not now wearing Mae Wests or carried the inflatable raft and I pictured many hungry sharks below in the somber waters. He made corrections toward shore each time I brought the error to his attention. I felt I could not stay awake any longer and pleaded to rest for the night at a motel and for my young life, as I felt I didn't have the strength to look out for us any longer. Absolutely he would not turn back a second time the same day. He needed to get back to work the coming morning. For the first time I took fate into my hands. Microphone in one hand, I dialed 121.7, the emergency frequency and very firmly announced, "if you will not consider to immediately land at the nearest airport, I will declare MAYDAY and that I am here against my will and better judgement." Without verbal response, at once the left wing dipped steeply as the Cessna made a 180-degree turn.

At the airport lobby we just dropped into the nearest comfortably oversized chairs, too exhausted to move. Rollie was very subdued, humbly he claimed, with my interference, I saved our lives. We landed in IFR conditions and a rough journey two days later in Rochester, but safe.

17 Aviation - Born to Fly e

Private Pilot Exam

THE LONG AWAITED moment had arrived. Rollie, my instructor, had finally given his OK for my flight test. It was customary for a flight instructor to give his consent. Although well prepared, I slept little the night before, as it had been my intention to pass the first time, not take repeated tests like many other pilots. Of course Rollie's pride as instructor and of his first and only woman student pilot was at stake.

9:00 A.M. sharp, apprehensively I entered the second story FAA office at Rochester airport. I was met by a man of medium height with squat and hostile appearance, who ordered me with a bark to take a seat at the only visitor chair. What was I doing here? Mr. Games, the head of the FAA, only gave exams for advanced IFR and commercial ratings. Maybe this is a fluke, I thought.

The twenty-minute oral private pilot exam was to begin. Mr. Games in a hoarse, harsh voice tossed at me the question to define the center of gravity of my plane. I do not remember whether I took our Cessna or Irv's, a friend and Rollie's student as well, brand new Cherokee. By now I was so nervous, my words just stumbled out incoherently. I knew the answer but chocked on my words. May I draw a diagram? This harsh retort startled me. "And what do you think this is, a drawing class?" I pulled myself together and thereafter responded softly to question after question he shot at me for a straight hour. Then I hit a snag I wasn't prepared for. "What is the horsepower of your plane?" Naively I thought out loud. "Cars have horsepowers. I didn't think of planes having horsepower." I ventured, "it is called a 180 Cherokee, so I suppose that must mean the horsepower." With a big mean grin he said, "look it up in the flight manual." Sure enough, that was it, 180 horsepower. Abruptly Mr. Games announced that he wanted to start the flight test.

I had conveniently parked the plane in front of the FAA building as was also instructed. Now I walked around it making a ground check, explaining everything I was checking out. I opened the hood and stuck my head into the engine compartment and explained what I was looking at, like no frayed wires. When I climbed into the pilot in command seat, my gruff examiner took the co-pilot seat. Ground control directed me towards the active runway. As I made my preflight check short of the runway, I made a last turn right and left looking for possible undetected aircraft coming in for a landing. I made a request for take off, simultaneously activating my flight plan, which I had prepared in the examiners office.

I had never flown to this destination. Flying next to this gruff and hostile man made me feel so apprehensive that I only flew by instinct, certain that I was to fail. I couldn't think or feel. Some quiet time later he elatedly shouted above the engine roar, "we're right above the airport, your cross country flying certainly has paid off." Next I was handed a black mask, which blocked the skyline and only allowed me to fly instruments. This procedure was supposed to be a five-minute exercise for the private pilot exam. I was comfortable and experienced just flying by instruments but the time I spent under the hood now was more like twenty minutes.

I do not remember all the exercises I was instructed to perform. It seemed I never had been taught some of this air work. Much time was spent doing emergency landings. I enjoyed the challenge of doing emergency landings, but now doing maneuvers, suddenly, he pulled the throttle and I was told exactly in which field I was to land. When I confidently approached for landing, he applied partial power so I overshot my intended landing spot again and again. At one point I got mad and tried to pry his huge hand off the throttle. To no avail. He kept an iron grip on the control. Never did I do as many emergency landings in succession.

Past noon, with a gruff bark, Mr. Games demanded I contact Rochester Tower for landing instructions. A private pilot flight exam should have taken no more than an hour, but this had taken more than twice that time. I landed and Ground Control guided me to the FAA building. The inspector got out of the plane while I quietly inquired if it was all right to head for the gas pit to refuel, as I had been taught the importance of immediately refueling after every flight. No, he wanted me to do one more go around, alone.

I was exhausted. My back was totally covered with perspiration as I rarely showed signs of overheating. Obediently I complied. Back in line with other aircraft, I waited for clearance from the tower. I wondered why was I asked for a "touch and go." I've performed those countless times. Throttle totally advanced, with full power the plane beckoned for take-off. I stayed in the pattern. 'Base leg' - 'downwind' then requested a final landing. No answer. The radios had always worked. Again I offered, "Rochester Tower - this is Cherokee 8483 Whisky - request landing instructions." Silence. Now utterly exhausted, I panicked and more urgently requested a landing. At the intersection of turning 'final' before allowed a landing my last effort was to let the tower know that I intended to leave the pattern and controlled air space for lack of communication, dipping my right wing into a 90 degree turn. What next? I would reenter the pattern with only light signals if the radios were still malfunctioning or land at Miller Field. This small airstrip was out of the way.

No this I didn't really want to do. Last spring, at the end of the rainy season, my instructor, for his own reasons, had asked me to check in at that airport. He wanted me to contact the guys at the office by radio to hear if the field was safe enough to land. "honey - come on down, we're all dry" was the response. Nevertheless circling the field at low altitude, seemed OK. Coming in slow and raising the nose high, I sunk deep into the turf and came to an abrupt halt. Almost instantly the guys were at my side. Much concerned, "honey are you alright?" I was embarrassed, the only woman pilot in the area, and I got stuck in the mud. But things could have been worse, I could have tipped over and broken the wings. It had taken several weeks for the field to dry out sufficiently to fly the Cessna to home base.

Again - very calmly, but loud and clear, a welcome voice, "this is Rochester Tower - Cherokee 8483 Whisky, cleared for landing." Immediately, abruptly I pulled the plane back to final, acknowledging much relieved, "Cherokee 8483 Whisky – Roger" and proceeded for landing. Chucks - chucks, before me, the gleaming silvery hull of an airliner that must have gotten permission for a straight in landing. Ordinarily I would have requested a go around, much simpler for a small craft than to land in jet stream with a good possibility to flip over. Surely the inspector was taking in the scene from his second floor office window with binoculars. Due to the previous communication problems I opted to land. The large, bright red letters spelled out AMERICAN AIRLINES at eye level. I pulled the throttle back gently, carefully slowing down the plane some more. Too slow would be dangerous at this low altitude. I tried to gain time before setting down in the jet stream. I wanted to show off a beautiful smooth landing but I knew it would be bumpy. I slowed up as much as I safely could, stalling, bouncing hard right at the beginning of the runway, where I wanted to touch down, to gain distance from the disturbing air stream. I took the first exit off the active, communicating, "Rochester ground control, request taxi instructions to the FAA building."

At 12:45 PM I parked once more in front of the FAA office, shutting down the engine. Mr. Games was standing in the doorway as he met me with the biggest grin, stretching out a muscular arm. He shook my hand and simply informed me that I had passed.

Once I was back home, I did what I never did during the day. From sheer exhaustion, I went to bed. The phone rang. It was my proud instructor - husband congratulating me on passing with the examiner's words, "with flying colors." Now it came to light, that due to his former student Irv passing only at his fourth try and at a small airport, Rollie was up for reexamination of his instructor license if his next student had failed. So I was sent to take my test to the head of the FAA who only conducted Instrument and Commercial pilot exams. I was awed. I had passed the commercial oral and flight test. Irv called next to congratulate me, as he had insisted on my using his brand new Cherokee for the exam, the plane I loved to fly and felt so comfortable with. I respected his showing genuine joy at my getting my license first try.

18 The Soviet Union a

Art

1965, THIS WAS the time I commenced seriously studying fine art. It was a bleak period in my life. I was often ill, seeking doctor's help, but no one was able to diagnose an ailment. This at the height of my youth. Depression left me with little energy or desire. By all standards I was well married and lived in a fashionable home in Rochester's beautiful suburbia. Kodak's film conventions enabled us to travel to Quebec, New York, Washington DC and California, ultimately to Europe and the Soviet Union.

Yet it was a time I was seeking more meaning for my personal existence. I was seeing Dr. Broida, a psychoanalyst for depression for years, but nothing seemed to help, although infrequent trips to New York always sparked renewed interest for life. Yes, I longed to return to New York. Rochester was Rollie's world, but he would not set me free. Most of my time I spent alone, or meeting briefly with friends over lunch, but later I felt betrayed by all. I was in deep physical and mental pain. I would often break down lie on the floor, or some sidewalk, ravaged with abdominal pain. I was seeking freedom but was kept caged.

I did enjoy the courses at Rochester Institute of Technology, working towards a Fine Arts degree, majoring in printmaking. But this ended too soon. Dr. Barkin, the head of the Art school, plus my instructors singled me out for my advanced work. Professor Barkin assigned me credit for previous studies at Traphagen School of Fashions and for studies in Berlin and Paris, plus hands-on experiences as an illustrator and fashion designer in the commercial field. All these credits were heaped upon me when I just got started, and I was informed that I was to graduate before too long.

Our split - level home had a beautiful studio addition with lovely views into our property full of trees overlooking a stream. When I felt better, I tried to draw and paint. Yet I couldn't work. I could not find any motivation or inspiration. As I had not yet fully realized, I was a colorist initially influenced with New York's school of Abstractionists. Here I felt stifled, expected to produce the usual realistic, but to me bland colored landscapes. For too long I felt listless. This was the end of my twenties, but I was not yet ready to give up on life, adapting to a boring useless bourgeois lifestyle. An artist has to feel free - think free - transact free to create unconcerned works. Inhale - then exhale.

A new seed planted itself into my mind. Seeking more creativity and perhaps freedom, I searched for freelance fashion design work in New York City. This I succeeded in doing from Rochester as my base, simultaneously keeping closer contact with the city galleries and museum happenings. I discovered I was happiest in turmoil of creative activities. Local exhibits of modest scale kept me occupied, and I started producing and showing my kind of work.

18 The Soviet Union b

ROLLIE HAD NOW finally consented to an uncontested divorce, so as not to make him look the guilty party, just in case he should want to remarry. His attorney friend Lloyd A. was to prepare the separation. At this time Eastman Kodak planned to partake in the International Congressional meetings in the Soviet Union. Almost immediately he regretted his consent to the divorce. Following the meetings, he wanted to tour the European Continent, his first exposure. Remembering my skills as interpreter during our South American tour, he baited me with the fine art collections of the renowned Hermitage Museum in Leningrad, now renamed from the former St. Petersburg.

I recalled stories of my adventurous grandfather Hugo Kühlich's business trips to St. Petersburg. Yes, I could be persuaded to attend this meeting and become acquainted with Russian art. In the past, volunteering graciously, I had contributed some German translations of various documents for Kodak, as wife of an employee, not realizing at the time that I would become valued for my translating ability and as go–between with the USA and German delegation in Moscow.

Our visas for Russia arrived and shortly thereafter Rollie and I departed. June 6, 1967, we flew into Paris. There were preliminary meetings while I was free to explore. My international group of friends of five years ago had dispersed back to their home countries. Only Mlle Lenoir, the kind seamstress of Jacques Heim, had remained. My French needed practice, but we eloquently conversed. I introduced Rollie to the Viscount and

Viscountess de Ricci, whose three children I had tended as governess, but now with a fourth child, they had nearly matured. It was a fun reunion and to Rollie's benefit English was spoken. The children each enjoyed their present from America. We received a gracious invitation to stay at their country home in the south of France. Regretfully our time did not allow us to detour.

On my own, I visited the Luykx family in Bruxell, and saw their pride of a newly constructed villa still in progress. In Amsterdam I briefly connected with Jacques, who had gotten married, and was happy with a baby daughter. At night we took in the hot spots of the town with friend Leo. In Frankfurt I was to pick up the pale blue Saab, ordered from the States. It was a joy to take in the idyllic southern German countryside. On my way to Vienna, I visited Jochen, former Berlin pal now still immersed in studies, working as a part time judge in Ansbach. He too now had a family, and we animatedly conversed of his recent experiences in Czechoslovakia. As we talked amiably over the evening meal around a large antique round table, I was the rare visitor from America, arriving in a brand new Saab. This was an occasion for a broad round–about discussion and many questions until late into the night. The following morning, with still many miles to cover to Vienna airport, only with luck, I caught Aeroflot for Moscow in time.

Primarily Russians were aboard as I detected only their language spoken. Seats were cramped and an unfamiliar odor permeated the cabin. I deducted it must be the insufficient pressurized air. I felt ill. After much delay, I arrived at the Moscow Airport. My husband was nowhere to be seen. Idly I stood around. Instead a Russian interpreter named Lara from the congress assigned to assist Rollie had come to meet me. She was tall, large boned but was made up in an attractive more Western style outfit and wearing makeup, unusual for the Russian women I had seen. When an announcement was made who I was, she stepped forward, dazzled at my petite frame and youthful attractiveness. Rollie being older, I was sometimes taken for his daughter. Lara said she had been waiting for my arrival for many hours. Shyly presenting me with a bouquet of flowers, explaining that they had wilted during the long wait. I deducted that she must have been one of many agents, hired to try to seduce members of the international team, and she was only doing her best. It was a job, but she seemed awed by her competition, the wife. Our divorce was to be finalized when we returned to the United States, so it no longer mattered to me. I kindly smiled at her and told her I was delighted she came for me, and thanked her for the thoughtfulness of the lovely flowers.

At our high-rise hotel, we overlooked the spread of Moscow with the prominence of the winding Volga. A pale blue sky, an overall very pale ambiance dominated all. Our photographs later to be developed were to attest to this transparent veil. Silently we motioned to one another as we bemusedly searched furniture for recording devices. Our conversation was guarded and only outdoors did we feel free to speak undetected by recording devices or personal guides.

We had to eat. Restaurants were sparse and dinner served at the hotel consumed many hours. We all met in the stately entrance hall, where many new acquaintances and reunions of former associates were made. Here again I met Alex Alden, Rollie's boss with his wife Florence, who on a side trip had independently explored the Black Sea. There was an abundance of heaping trays of caviar served with white bread and ravaged by all. Of the time consuming dinner, later I would only recall eating *borscht*, beef with red beets and very tasty.

Negotiations with the German delegates were not running smoothly. I was surprised by a meeting with Dr. Fröngel, my father's former associate from their Rissen partnership. My command of both languages, German and English at the time was fluent and much appreciated. I went to see the sights with my private guides, a young law student plus our driver, presumably another agent. I was only shown what I was supposed to be informed about. After spending many hours in a gallery showing only somber looking male portraits, I was making requests of what I was interested in. My young student guide agreeably made a request for the driver to take us to the outskirts of Moscow. The driver seemed the superior but did not speak English. A fierce argument ensued in Russian, whereby the older driver physically shoved about the young student. He later confessed to me that the government was in control of his life and that he was not assured a position as an attorney after graduation. Rather, he would be assigned a position wherever he was needed, in whatever capacity.

I was totally disinterested in what I was allowed to see. It was still the time of the Iron Curtain, a lead weight separating East from West. For whatever small offenses, one could be imprisoned without Western influence of a fair trial. I was young and adventuresome and Rollie being preoccupied with lengthy meetings, I set out on my own. With just a few rubles I headed for the subway. I could see very few automobiles on Moscow's wide avenues, which were mainly for government use and a few taxis, all of old vintage.

None of the visitors got the experience of the underground. An architectural masterpiece in marble, each station was individually beautifully designed, nothing like the dingy New York subway. Without a guide I was very visibly the foreigner and

vulnerable. With my slender build, colorful contemporary wardrobe, heavy make-up and long straight hair I had all attention. I
had made some last minute preparations to learn the language,
but the alphabet alone presented a hurdle.

Women came up close to me with admiring glances eager
with questions but it was difficult to communicate. One heavy
set woman gently stroked my hair. It soon turned out to be a
challenge identifying the names of the stations as we sped by. I
had a map and we were heading for the suburbs, but I was not
sure where I thought I should be. I left the train and the station
to wander about looking for help. An Engineer approached me
speaking German. He was so happy to be practicing his German,
then considered a second language in Russia, and to be conversing with a Westener, a rare treat. He and his companions and
I had a long and animated conversation. I had to answer many
questions about the Western world, and they were freely talking about the state of the common people, their hardships and
frustrations. I did get to the outskirts of town, seeing all-women
teams performing manual hard labor. I was told a shortage of
labor forced women to build roads and dig ditches. They were
seen at every building site but not working in town. Kind words
and directions got me back to the hotel in time for the caviar hors
d'oevres.

A recommended attraction was the glass tomb preserving
Lenin. Long lines of Russian tourists, from far reaches of that
vast country, on vacation, extended from the Lenin Square. With
some guilty feelings on my part, the guide walked me right up
front to the tomb, yet people smiled, willingly making space for
me all in the name of diplomacy while they must have been waiting for many hours. It was awesome how lifelike he was in an aura
of peace, and how incredibly well preserved the figure rested.

Nearby on Moscow's Red Square were the much-admired colorful ornately fashioned onion towers of St. Basil's Cathedral, and
within their treasures of religious icons.

Then Leningrad, on the Gulf of Finland, in clear view facing Finland, was truly enjoyable for me. It had been reclaimed
from the swamp lands, and many canals still flowed through what
was to be again proud St. Petersburg. We first visited Peter the
Great's delightful former summer Palace, Petrodvorets. Then it
was pure ecstasy for me, to view the multitude of native and international art treasures in the Czars Winter Palace, now called
the Hermitage Museum, in the midst of town. We saw ornate
high ceilinged banquet halls with the most exquisite wooden inlaid floors, itself an art. Of most interest to me were the halls of
German masters. So much of the art I found missing in the Berlin
and other major German city museums could be viewed here in
vast quantities. Sadly I found the moisture saturated walls and
ceilings had done much damage to these masterpieces. The magnificent inlaid floors were badly scarred and punctured. Despite
the sobering effect of lack of maintenance, here was one of the
world's foremost art collections. Indeed it was the highlight of
my trip.

Alex Alden was secretary of Motion Picture and Television
Engineers, for Twentieth Century Fox. He chaired the convention
of the International Congress in Russia. Much later our roads would
cross again, and he was to become a close friend. He was born in
Russia of noble descent. The Bolshevik lead Revolution executed
the Zsar Nicholas Romanov and the nobility and ruling classes.
Alex, as a young child succeeded in escaping the country with his
mother princess L, a nurse, with some close friends who chose the
route of their exit via the Orient. They settled in California. Now
as a technical delegate, representing the United States, this was

his first and only return to his former homeland. His identity of a once prominent family must have surely been known. Alex always stayed calm, thus this journey must have been a very sensitive reunion. Shortly after his return to the US he suffered a heart attack. He survived and lived close to his 90th year.

After our departure from the Soviet Union we picked up the Saab at the Vienna airport and headed straight for Rollie's ancestral Czechoslovakia, of which he was second-generation immigrant. Like other Russian satellites, this Balkan country was also under iron Soviet domination. The family had kept in touch with the US relatives. One Zavada was an established poet, whose poetry was recited in the schools. Another relative was fortunate to live in a tiny modern apartment, but the walls were already crumbling. His wife was a doctor, they had a small child, but even with two incomes, it was all they could afford. Another young threesome family had to stay with in-laws in cramped quarters. Relatives had once held high positions in government before the change of power, we learned that their descendants were denied an education. Much ado was made of this former migrant and a meeting was staged in a theater where Rollie gave a talk and many questions were raised. For some reason it was insisted that I too join him on stage. Prague was a picturesque town with cobble-stoned streets but sadness was impressed on the faces and the demeanor among the inhabitants. This was my last deep down depression as I felt the pain of these valiant people, a like fate of all Balkans. I yearned to cross the Austrian border into the free world.

In romantic Heidelberg, I had to visit a doctor due to a strep throat, I figured caused by stress. The doctor spent much time with me in lively conversation, a rare American patient just having returned from behind the iron curtain. Following that we enjoyed a boat ride down the Rhine, departing from Köln, sipping local wine produced by the vineyards we passed on both sides of the river. Then we had a brief encounter with the snow-capped Alps on treacherously narrow winding mountain roads of Switzerland.

In Lübeck I saw my grandmother for the last time. She stayed in a beautiful and modern old age home surrounded by a rose garden. She bemoaned the fact that she missed her freedom in

**Last visit with grandmother in Lübeck, Germany
on return from Russia in 1967**

the Rissen apartment we once all shared. *Tante* Eva, her oldest daughter discovered that she had saved up a sizable amount of money while checking through her papers. The children decided at ninety-two she deserved to live in more comfort. Not long after checking into the home, still in excellent health, she departed peacefully in her sleep.

From Travemünde by ferry in the North Sea, we headed for wonderful – wonderful Copenhagen and the delight of Tivoli Gardens. There were debriefing meetings in London. Just before our return to the States, we took time to visit my British relatives, the Ayeling's. Dagmar and Laurence had turned into very independent teenagers and I still enjoyed their British accents. Uncle Jack had never flown, so we surprised him by renting a small plane to take him and *Tante* Asta to skirt the Leigh-on-Sea coast. It is something he had wanted to experience, but during flight they both looked apprehensive and turned somewhat pale as we banked over the ocean. I believe they were very happy to touch ground again. In all, for me this unforeseen trip was a memorable experience.

19 A Career Takes Off a

AT THE END of July, Lloyd, the attorney and friend of Rollie, was preparing the documents I was to take to Ciudad Juárez, Mexico the following month, barely making the deadline for ending Mexican quick divorces. I flew into El Paso, the final day for this supposedly uncontested and painless procedure. That day was a big hype with ample news coverage. Another young woman, a brunette, and I, the blond, were singled out. A journalist photographer requested our permission to document this last day of instant divorce procedure.

Under other circumstances we might have relished being in the limelight. Every word and every one of our opinions was recorded on film and with pen. We were treated royally and kept comfortably separate from the crowd. With the mayor, town officials, and media, we were invited to lunch in one of the finest restaurants. Rollie called, because he was still trying to change my mind about the divorce while I was on Mexican soil, as he continued to do for the coming ten years.

With the divorce finalized, I arrived back in New York City that very night. Once again I checked into the YWCA, hoping for success by starting with a modest beginning. I was gripped with fear, having comfortably lived in the affluent Rochester suburb, that I would not succeed in a competitive profession. Humbly starting at the "Y", I figured, one could only "go up" and improve one's lot.

Fate must have played a role, as I found an apartment on 82nd Street and Riverside Drive, my old neighborhood. It was a narrow apartment building with a dozen floors. I occupied a studio apartment on the 7th floor, bright and clean, which accommodated the few belongings I now owned. My only expense was purchase of a Castro Convertible pull out couch. The window stretched the whole expanse of the narrow room, facing the classic New York brown stone houses across the street and exposing part of Riverside Park greenery. In due time, a shipment arrived of boxes such as my introductory paintings, art supplies, books and some kitchen utensils.

In a couple of weeks I was working on 7th Avenue, and my choice was sportswear. Incredible. With a five-year gap of fashion experience, again I worked in my chosen field. Mostly I surprised myself, with ideas coming quicker than I was able to sketch them down. Sportswear had been my favorite *métier,* and my children's, teens and ladies swim wear designs sold well, keeping our six factories running day and night. I was appreciated and most of all I loved what I was doing, each morning eager to rise and head for the garment industry to create. Dave G. Inc. was on the 23rd floor, my glass enclosed design studio scanning the high rises and in view of the boating activities on the Hudson River. I kept so busy that I took hardly time for this spectacular panorama. I was well compensated and according to my accountant, "you make too much money", and was placed into the top income bracket for women in the US. Women at that time had much lower incomes than men. But as the immigrant, I felt I had succeeded in obtaining job satisfaction and adequate pay for the first time, being able to afford my heart's desires, modest as they were. Well paying freelance designing jobs materialized as well, as the sale ability of my fashions became acknowledged.

To satisfy other creative desires, again I signed up at the well known Art Students League for night courses, as I felt a surge of energy and compulsion to produce fine art along with my commercial design. This time I could afford my classes and did not need to expend time and energy on modeling to compensate tuition. Even on my job I now declined modeling to clients like Macy's, Sears, Montgomery Ward, Lerner Bros., since I was successfully selling and that I thought adequate. My designs were copied. I spotted long rows of knock offs I spotted at Macy's and other stores. Even delivery trucks on the highway were twice high-jacked. A friend, who now too wanted to try her luck at fashion designing, was interviewed identifying herself in my name. It came back to me and I thought it a compliment.

I studied with Theodoros Stamos, an abstract expressionist, and a very exciting and productive period evolved for me. I started to produce large canvases in bright colors, interpretations of nature. I worked five nights at the League and once a week Stamos showed up to critique our works. With much apprehension I would present my paintings, as each of us did, the whole class at attention to benefit his critiques. We greatly benefitted from each other's presentations. I recall that Stamos would beg for silence, as we'd stumble, trying to explain our works. "Painter paint, let your work speak for itself," he'd counsel each of us. Most students were obsessed with copying their favorite master. I was the only one with an independent style and was rewarded with a good critique about my individual technique. I received strong advice to keep on painting.

A year later I felt the need to work from the figure in larger format and changed instructors. Then I knew I had my own style and that I was a colorist. We worked directly from the model onto canvas in oil or acrylic and some exciting pieces came from that period. Instructor Green used a limited palette of black, gray and white. I experimented in this limited color scheme but it didn't work for me. Still I was happy at the League working out my ideas. Green took me aside and explained that he had nothing more to teach me. He admired my expertise with the figure, my individuality in design and use of color. I had graduated. He set me free. Complimented though I felt, I knew I'd miss my friends and the atmosphere of the League. My independence and love of modernism characterized the beginning of a new endeavor. With the easel centered in my small apartment, I went to work, creating a number of large canvases, later to be exhibited in galleries and museums.

Accumulating a body of paintings in my small studio apartment caused a problem of storage. It was time to expose myself to the public, and it was fun showing in-group exhibits on East 57th Street and Madison Avenue. I even sold some works. Life was good.

19 A Career Takes Off b

Play Time

I WAS STARTING to feel the stress of the responsibility to produce salable styles to keep the factories running. Mr. Gold the owner gave me an excellent review at the end of my first season. In the thirty-year history of the company, my designs achieved the highest sales. In a more serious tone, I was advised that even better sales were expected of me for the coming season, and every season to come. So I kept doing my very best.

Mr. Gold spent much time playing golf, frequently taking off long weekends heading for Florida, and I was generously expected to take time off as well. My small studio apartment took little time to maintain. It was wonderful for the first time to be able to afford art supplies and necessities as need or desire arose. I combed the art galleries and museums to be inspired by the masters for new techniques and styles. Now painting on my own, aside from commercial projects, I prepared for a future passion in fine art.

With more leisure and the means to pursue my hobbies, I started playing tennis on public courts. I went on weekend ski trips to upstate New York Hunter, Bellaire, and in Vermont Mt. Snow, Bromley. At times I was the ski instructor, which compensated for my trips. Still frugal, I liked the idea of my costly hobbies being self-supporting. A couple of summers I explored with friends the rugged coast of Maine in *Rowdy II*, a 40-foot sailboat. July, when waters were still icy, we started with a clam bake in Ilsboury Island and from there sailed to

Seal Harbor, Hog Island, stayed in dense fog on Monhegan Island which had an art colony, then Rockland and back to Dark Harbor. Other trips exploring the New England coast-line added to summer joys.

It was the first death in my immediate small north American family. My mother called that Bruno, her husband, beloved to our small clan, had unexpectedly passed away of a heart attack. Bruno's death should not have been so unexpected had I been more sensitive to his increasing weakness and an earlier close call of an attack. Mr. Gold was hesitant to allow me some days off for the funeral to the remote north Canadian settlement on the Georgian Bay.

Bruno Löffler had immigrated with his wife, shortly after the war from heavily bombed out Berlin to carve a new life in the Canadian wilderness. He was a machinist and took great pride in his work. His only son, Bodo, was born in Canada, and his mother passed away soon after. Bruno's death was a great loss to us all, yet I was happy to briefly leave the big city and unite with my family.

At this funeral and at other visits, I looked the alien to this isolated small conservative community. Flying from New York to Toronto, then taking a bus north was a complicated journey. Tall and super thin in a stylish ankle length, tight fitting wool coat, stylish high boots and with my long light colored windblown hair, I was nicknamed *the blond witch*. A local newspaper reporter splashed a story of this metropolis fashion designer and global traveler.

I enjoyed this back country as much as big city living. When I could I visited my mother. She was now alone, not comprehend-ing the language well, never having learned to drive a car; she was lonely. On my visits as well by mail I helped with her paper work. Once with a pilot friend we flew a Cessna up to this frozen winter wonderland.

I also loved to ski. Designing a successful line of sportswear for the coming season, I felt the intense pressure. I needed playtime. Sensational skiing in Aspen, Colorado, caught my eye. I treated myself to a pair of *Rosignol* racing skis, which Jean Claude Killey, the Olympic champion promoted. Winter was our slow selling season and it was a good time to take a vacation. Dave Gold showed a kindly smile, and said "where do you intend to go?" With my response to take a group ski-tour to Aspen, his benevolent smile instantly clouded. He had to think about it. First thing the coming morning he confronted me in my studio that he had called a meeting and it was unanimously decided that I could not ski. Specially trained for this job, should I be injured, I could not easily be replaced. With new skis, a new outfit, I could afford to ski the magnificent Rockies - and now it was considered too dangerous for me. My phone and studio were *tagged*, listened to, I had to be careful to express my shattered feelings. An exception was made to allow me to fly. I was downhearted and perhaps did not hide well my sadness. This trip meant so much to me. Some days later Mr. Gold approached me with a broad smile and offered that it was OK for me to take that trip, with a stern warning though to be extra careful skiing.

The trip was all I had dreamed of. It was a blast. A full week skiing these magnificent powdered trails was pure bliss. It even crossed my mind to become a full time ski instructor or a happy ski bum, if it weren't for the fact that I didn't want to forego my New York based responsibilities. The ski group was fun. The trails were a challenge. Skiing powder for the first time was the next best thing to heaven I imagined.

Back at my New York design studio, well rested, I produced

an abundance of styles of high approval and sales. Pleased with my surge of creative output, Mr. Gold confided that I would have the freedom in the future to take a vacation anytime and keep my own schedule as long as I completed the line of new seasonal styles on time. Everyone was happy. I now regularly skied weekends in Vermont, either teaching, sometimes racing or just in company of friends.

On one of these ski trips I met Jerry von Grote, 6'4", lean and handsome and coincidentally born in East Germany. The occasion was an evening social with dancing. His ski club and my group connected. Speaking the same language was an instant attraction. Thereafter Jerry came frequently for visits to New York and later to my New Jersey flat. The weekend after our meeting, I was injured when a student crashed into me, causing a concussion. My head and eyes turned blue-black. Wearing sunshades, I did not miss a day of work.

The invasion of cockroaches into my snug apartment became most unbearable. My landlord would spray the apartment and the critters escaped to the neighboring flats. When their places were sprayed the roaches returned to me in even greater numbers. When I returned in the evening and turned on the lights, the sink was black with roaches as they scurried away. They had gotten into my food, clothing, bedding - everywhere. It was time to move. Across the East River in North Bergen, New Jersey, I found a spacious modern apartment, right at the river with views of the Manhattan skyline. Life was a blast.

19 A Career Takes Off c

Staten Island - CAP

LIFE HAD BEEN settled well enough. My apartment was sufficient. I had a job I was excited about, and again in a serious way,
I commenced painting. Yet a hunger wasn't stilled. Every time
I would look into the blue sky, and see a small aircraft cheerily
gliding about, nestled deep within the big cities skyscrapers, my
heart would ache. I missed flying. So one Saturday morning, I
took myself to Westchester airport to check out their Cherokees,
wanting, with a bird's eye view, to acquaint myself with the New
York area. I loved to fly the sporty low wing Cherokees. I tried
to justify the expense of this costly hobby by saying I had a high
stress job and needed to work out my problems. From that lofty
vantage point, earthly troubles seemed insignificant.

One day I took a friend flying, Pete, who'd never been in a
small plane. Pre-flighting the Cherokee I found the brakes were
not working right. I requested another plane. While we waited at
the rental plane, a young man hurried over to Pete. "Yes sir, what
can I do for you, sir?" Pointing to me, Pete said that I was the
pilot. Condescendingly the young man turned to me, "the plane
works perfectly well, you don't need brakes to fly." "After touch
down, one needs brakes to slow up leaving the active, runway"
I responded. "If you do not have a plane in good working condition I'll head over to Teterboro." And so I did. Teterboro rented
Cessnas.

So for weekends I would check weather and then reserve
their standard Cessna 160. Sometimes I would invite a friend

to partake in the joy of a local flight above the Hudson River. One friend, Sherry had never flown before and tried to conceal her fright. While pre-flighting the plane, another pilot just having tied down his plane after completion of his flight, walked over to us and with a big grin offered, "Yikes, two women." Once airborne and out of the airport's control zone, I gave Sherry the experience of handling the controls. She loved her first flying venture and later confessed her increased fear after the fellow's comment. When parting at the Manhattan subway for our apartments, she came forth with, "Barbara, you forgot something." Cheerily she said, "you forgot to invite me for another flight."

Indeed, Teterboro at that time, was considered the busiest airport in the country for private pilots. Sometimes one would have to hold in the pattern for up to twenty minutes, flying a tight turn in a tower-designated area at low altitude, a very dangerous ordeal in a buzzing airport. Very few women were flying those days. So my female voice with an accent must have had the tower operators overly concerned. Invariably, almost instantly, I would be granted permission to land just to get me out of the dense traffic maze. I felt capable handling the traffic but didn't mind preferential treatment now, while being bored flying tight circles. Perhaps it may have been considered prejudice toward the weaker sex.

During those New York winters I would ski in Vermont. In spring I got back to flying and after a three months absence of flying, one was required a check - out. At one time a commercial pilot, who loved to associate himself with small aircraft in his spare time, gave me the check - ride. It was a very windy day; student pilots were not permitted to fly. A check out flight was to last about an hour, and I was pleased that I was able to prove myself in half the time, being told, that I was very safe.

One early Saturday I slipped into my bright orange flight suit, on the collar sporting my wings, a small pin designating a pilot, destination CAP, Civil Air Patrol. First I walked a couple of blocks to the West side subway station, changing at Times Square for the lower East side subway. Then a ferry would take me across the Sound to Staten Island. There I'd wait for a bus, direction "Miller Air Force field," and upon arriving, I had still a few blocks to walk. So finally I passed the gate of the military field searching for the Civil Air Patrol building.

My arrival met with absolute disbelief. A woman in a flight suit. Obviously I looked official. When the middle aged colonel took sight of me, his face turned bright red, then a shade of deep purple. Without a welcome or a single word, he abruptly left the office to take the stairs to his upper office sanctuary. The major, second in command, warmed up some to my presence and so did the other pilots after their the first jolt. I placed my gold embossed logbook before the major while filling out forms. The major never opened my logbook, which was in plain view, to acquaint himself with my experience. Later, I understood that my fate already had been determined.

Apprehensive of my every step in this new group, I almost overlooked the warmth and admiration of the young cadet's. These young girls and women had joined CAP in a patriotic spirit and a dream of flying. As a woman aviatrix in a flying suit, I represented their heroine. When I wasn't kept busy with paperwork, tests and check flights, the girls would assemble around me with a multitude of questions. How did I do it? They all aspired to be like me. One young woman confided that she saved every cent she could from her waitressing job to take flying lessons.

Curiosity ran high about this female pilot. A handsome young checkout pilot, a lieutenant, straight away took me to their pride and joy, a Cessna 182, for the check ride. I had taken many check rides and flown in stressful adverse conditions, so this seemed routine. The Lieutenant took this matter very seriously, while the whole crew watched with binoculars or bare eye. Abruptly he would put the plane onto its wing, into a stall or spin from which I was to recover. During all these maneuvers I realized quickly that he was ambitious and tried to provoke my fear and ineptitude. As under all circumstances, I do my best. But in his ambition to prove me incompetent, I was watching out for our safety and would not allow the plane to get into too dangerous maneuvers. He wanted to know what work I did. Translated - how could I afford to fly. He could not comprehend that a fashion designer earned an income to afford costly pastimes. The landing did prove a challenge. Base leg took me over the high school, where he taught and asked me always to be very cautious on approach. Miller Air Force Base had two runways, one for military aircraft and the other runway paralleled for use of Civil Air Patrol. Our runway was short; a tall wire fence hovered between the high school and the start of the runway. At the end of the runway was the two-story CAP building. One had to be high enough on approach to clear the wire fence, dip down onto the runway without picking up extra speed, slow up quickly so as not to hit the CAP building. The lieutenant wasn't happy, but he had to report that I was very safe.

Since I loved to fly it didn't seem to matter much to me whether these maneuvers were legal, but I was sent up for two more check – rides with other pilots, who worked me hard. Same results, I had to be passed. There were a number of pilots and only one plane, so we each had a short spell to ourselves. It was great flying on my own. The New York skyline was magnificent. Then there was Long Island, the Sound, and the Atlantic

Ocean. There were challenges flying out of Miller Field, like restricted air spaces at different altitudes. One day of unfavorable winds down the short runway had me squirming. I could not land and quickly, partway down the runway I decided for a go around. The second time I made the landing, noticing many binoculars pointing to my plane. I felt embarrassed that I didn't come to a full stop the first time. One benevolent pilot confessed that no one else could land the first time either.

The Colonel wasn't happy to have me one of the crew. Another time I had to crawl under the belly of the plane to check on something, getting my orange flight suit full of grease. Then the major took me aside for an oral test. I seemed to know all the answers. Colonel's orders were for every one to take a written test. Most pilots were older; many years had passed since ground school. I was the youngest and closest in years having prepared for my written exam. Devastating to the colonel and major, all pilots failed the test. I was the exception and so kept on flying.

One freezing early winter morning, I was the first to try for a flight. The Cessna wouldn't start. In Rochester I remembered putting blankets over the engine at night or using an electric heater. One could also start the engine by one person cranking the propeller and the other turning the ignition, a dangerous ordeal, as many a pilot had lost a finger or a hand. As luck would have it the Colonel was on hand. He cranked the propeller, while I in the cockpit with open window received his screaming demands. I was duly intimidated. I do not remember the details. The colonel turned red, shouting out my faults and disappeared. The Lutenant came to the scene, confiding that the plane couldn't get started and I did only what I was told. The Lutenant put his arm around me and confessed, that he and the other checkout pilots had orders to flunk me. The Colonel's words were, women belong in the kitchen. "Well, you just weren't flunkable," and he stated that I had proven to be a very safe pilot. From now on he offered to look out for me.

With all this hard flight training, I thought, I was considered very safe and then I should not need someone to look out for me. I was very young and naïve, "before my time" as it was called. A woman was still thought to need a man to look out for her. Since that day I have not soloed a plane. I regret, I didn't fight and let them down. All those young women cadets, their eyes set on me, whose dreams were to become pilots.

When I moved to the southwest, briefly staying in Arizona, the Ninety-niners invited me on a flight mission. I had never heard of this organization. It was originally initiated by ninety-nine women pilots internationally and headed by Amelia Earhart as its first president of the group. At their conventions, the Hilton and other fine hotels, they received free accommodations and the red carpets were spread out to this valiant sisterhood.

The president who invited me flew a smart looking sports plane, proudly stating that she had acquired it on her own. The co - pilot seat was taken by another guest, a sixteen-year-old, daughter of a Colonel who had just been awarded a scholarship to the U.S. Airforce Academy. I took the backseat, which rarely happened. A whole group of small planes departed Cottonwood airport, spiraling to a height to traverse Mingus Mountains, destination Wickenburg. Although it was a beautiful clear day, I noticed the pilot opted to fly IFR. She started squirming as instruments were malfunctioning; she couldn't receive the omni signals. I had been trained VFR, to fly by the seat of my pants. I wasn't worried as I knew the area and visually could direct us to the town.

The 99ers had made it one of their numerous missions to

paint in large letters the identity of some smaller airfields to guide errant pilots. When I flew, a pilot was expected to know where he was at all times. This service was appreciated by the airports, and we were served a free lunch. The young woman hovered close to me as we each painted with big brushes and rollers and in white paint. To the women about me I recounted my last CAP flying experience with the prejudiced Colonel. The young woman at my side softly responded, "thank you for having been there, without you I would not be here." I was duly touched. The 99ers would have come to my aid but unfortunately I didn't know they existed.

Many years later on September 11, 2001, we all witnessed the shocking demolition of New York's twin towers, an act that paralyzed this country and the world. Air traffic in New York came to a standstill with only Civil Air Patrol, always in the quiet background, collecting blood plasma, all medical supplies and handling emergency traffic. They were the unsung heroes.

PART III
Beginning Once More

20 Connecticut-Family-Another Career a

Connecticut

JERRY AND I saw one another most weekends, despite the distance between New York and Bridgeport, Connecticut. He worked for General Electric and part time he studied for his Masters degree in Business Administration. February 28th was our first date, in New York City. I had to wear dark shades to hide my bruised face and eyes due to a skiing accident, when a student collided into me. Two years later on February 29th, Leap Year, our daughter Erika was born. Subsequently she celebrated her birthdays respectively on the 28th.

All immigrants have their own distinct tale of trauma or reason for coming to the USA. Jerry's ancestors were knighted in the 13th century, living as well bestowed estate owners in Rostock, Mecklenburg, what was to become East Germany after World War II. His mother, Baroness Sabine von Kardorf was the only daughter of several sons who did not return from the war, with the exception of the eldest, a pilot. One of her brothers had brought home a friend for the holidays, Baron Gerhard von Grote. It was customary for nobility to marry within their own caste. Marriage of the only daughter to Baron von Grote was to be a big event. The servants of her parental estate were to enjoy this wedding, so musicians, the feast and personnel were brought by private train from Berlin for the ceremony to Rostock.

It was a happy short-lived marriage. Her husband, a test

pilot in the war, crashed his plane three months before his twin sons Gerhard and Klaus, were born two hours apart. Baroness Sabine had stayed on the parental estate with her twin sons. Servants tended to the children, as she was not accustomed to working.

The war ended with the Communists taking over the land, which became the new Eastern sector of Germany. All people performed forced labor. Especially singled out were the estate owners and nobility. Baron and Baroness von Kardorf, now in advanced age would have had to work the fields beside their former servants. The decision was made that they would take their own lives with their most trusted servant arranging the burial in the family cemetery. Baroness Sabine with her two young sons were ready to join her parents. But the parents strongly urged her for the sake of the boys to seek freedom in the Western zone and start a new life. Her escape west was then primarily for the children to live on and carry forth the family name.

After her parent's funeral, Sabine gathered some chests full of family treasures, jewelry, tapestries, fine embroidered linens and photographs. The loyal servants sent them off as she parted with some of the finest horses. An able horsewoman, the Baroness navigated only by night so as not to be detected by Communist soldiers. During daylight hours they would hide, rest or be on guard in the thickets of the woods.

Freedom in war torn West Germany was harsh living, which she was not accustomed to. Western sector relatives living on estates and in castles would not accept them, as they were barely able to feed themselves. The Grote's ended up in a refugee camp. To retain some privacy for her family, in a large room filled with many families, the Baroness would drape some cloth over a strung line. In this hopeless situation the decision was made to escape once more, now to the United States of America. Luck and the sale of the finely bred horses secured passage for the journey.

Arriving in the land of freedom, she was little prepared to fend for herself and her family. There were no relatives or friends awaiting and guiding her. She had no marketable skills. So she ended up in Bridgeport Connecticut, working a most menial shift in a factory and renting the small attic apartment I was to meet them in much later. As is the custom in the America, nobility is stripped of their titles, all living equally, now as commoners. Most immigrants arrive from a past of poverty or persecution, with the incentive of hard labor to do well. She only lived to raise her children, in total isolation, her spirit broken. Surrounding herself with family photographs, her memories were anchored to the past.

Klaus, the younger twin, in his mid twenties, was the first to return to the homeland, that is, West Germany. Meanwhile the family estate housed the East Sector government. Interior walls were torn out to accommodate offices and generally all was left to decay. Klaus stayed with relatives some time and married a German woman, a commoner. Both Jerry and his mother went to Germany for the wedding. Maggie was well liked by the Baroness as she was tall, stately, attractive with jet black hair just the color of her late husband. She was a secretary, just like the Baroness had been, though briefly.

Jerry invited me home. Not many visitors came to their dwelling. A narrow dark stairway led to the attic apartment, which had a couple of small and somber rooms with slanted walls. Our first few meetings were guardedly polite. As I learned later, she accepted none of her son's friends. I was no exception. At 5'6", I was too short, "a little shrimp" she retorted, blowing cigarette smoke into my face. I maintained a slender, elegant model figure, which was too thin for her liking. As a curly red head, she abhorred blonds. Of course she had no way of knowing, but as fashion designer I was in the top income bracket in the US, yet she looked down upon me as poor and low class. She confronted me alone, "after her son's friendships would end," as they always did, "he again would devote himself totally to her full-time." In a sense this proved to be correct.

20 Connecticut-Family-Another Career b

Connecticut – Family Life

I WAS READY to leave my roach infested apartment in New York. The ideal abode presented itself in North Bergen, New Jersey. It was a spacious bright contemporary studio with a patio overlooking the Hudson River. Across the street, luscious greenery stretched along for blocks with tennis courts. It was an easy commute to work.

This time again I was looking for more challenges. Skiing weekends in Vermont, I decided to pursue designing a line of skiwear. There was an interested business and even a financial partner. Now I was working up some sketches and reviewing freelance sewing factories. All this while I was still secure and happy designing sportswear. Life was good for the coming year.

Jerry and I were to be married. With a small salary, he was always indebted to his mother Sabine. We agreed to invest in a condominium. Of course mother had to look after her son's interest. She approved of the very first condo. Further she insisted, the property and all my financial assets had to be in the man's name. This was before we were married. I took Jerry aside to give him numerous reasons why this condo didn't seem right for us. Under their combined pressure, I signed the papers. After a sleepless night I contacted an attorney in New York. Yes, I was able to retreat from this deal. He also looked over my previous divorce papers and was infuriated by my having been financially so grossly taken advantage of. Due to getting remarried shortly, he did not want me pressured into opening a lawsuit against my former husband. He was a kindly man and further offered advice of keeping my professional name, as he considered me professionally accomplished in both my fashion and fine art career.

I was still working in New York, but we decided to live in Stamford, Connecticut, supposedly halfway between our jobs. We ended up renting a modest one-bedroom apartment. He drove his Pontiac to Bridgeport. I walked a short distance to the commuter train station. After an hour or sometimes two, depending on problems arising like fires, derailments, repairs, I'd arrive at Grand Central Station, New York. Then I'd continue by subway, another few blocks walk on the south end of the garment district, then up the troublesome, often stalling elevator to my twenty-third floor studio. After a busy workday plus twice this commuter scenario, I'd find a hungry husband impatiently waiting for his dinner.

Almost immediately I became pregnant. I felt nauseated and weak, barely able to motivate myself to handle the simplest chores. My gynecologist, with bored expression declared, "everything in the book is ailing you and nothing can be done about it." As I could not easily be replaced on my job, I didn't want to let my boss down. Courageously I continued to complete designing my last fashion line for some seven months to come. Feeling ill and weak, I had to abandon producing my own ski fashion line.

At thirty, Jerry felt he was too young to become a father. It was not a marriage he had anticipated. He was responsible for a new wife who was pregnant, ill, growing fat, and not catering to his every need like his mother had done. He wanted meals on time, and his shirts ironed, and resented being encouraged to share some house chores. He even challenged whether this

233

child was his. He asked what was I doing on those long train rides home? Darkest doubts were planted into his mind. With smug demeanor, his mother stepped again into the place of his closest confidante, as he had no friends.

When my line was completed, promptly, I was fired. In a glamorous profession as fashion designer, during the thirty year history of the company there had never been a married, much less a pregnant designer. I felt gratitude and relief. The son – mother team would not have allowed me to quit. Yet my unemployment check was higher than a secretary's salary. My kindly boss must have perceived the physical struggles I endured. Feeling ill with the stress of commuting and in emotional turmoil, I feared for the unborn's well being. Yes, I wanted this child. Gripped with fear of harm done to us and loss of my independence, I could in no way foresee fending for us both. I felt so utterly alone.

While at home, during the last few months of my pregnancy, I painted a series of stones on the small kitchen table. A former engagement of a solo painting exhibit inconveniently for February at Bartholomews Community Club in New York, kept me happily occupied. The opening was a pleasant respite as many old friends showed up to wish me well.

February 29th, 1972, our healthy leap-year daughter was born, named Erika. Jerry's initial joy turned into gloom, as his mother did not approve of a girl. This noble clan was at the verge of dying out and needed a male heir to continue the line. It was a difficult birth, and we stayed in the hospital for ten days. Sabine visited once, and with an unemotional mood, presented a box of German chocolates and observed, "you look just dreadful." On my first painful walk down the hospital corridor, Jerry commented, "you have do this again, you must bear a son." My thoughts were, "if I silently hang on, I'll destroy myself."

I enjoyed the beauty of Connecticut with its old historic charm and white-sandy beaches on the Long Island Sound. Fall brought a brilliant color spectrum of maples, birches, and oak trees. I walked the beaches and parks with the baby. We had picnics and swam. Time passed with new wounds instilled. The Grote clan published a paper in Germany, a yearly update of family events. Proudly the Baroness shared the good news of a new family addition and that Erika looked just like the father. Emotionally there was no respite as Sabine cleverly created new hurdles. One day, over the Sunday dinner I had prepared, she implored me to seek rest at a mental institution. I could commit myself and later, when I felt like it "come back to the outside world." European and eastern nobility often disposed of unwanted females to insane institutions. Oh yes, she and Jerry would easily take care of the baby. It broke the straw. Jerry would now see his mother alone. I did not need her presence and cutting remarks. I felt her wedge between us. Physically, one day he assaulted me and I remembered witnessing the beatings my mother received from my father. As a young child I had vowed never to let a man abuse me this way. Jerry was 6'4" and very strong, while I was 5'6" very slender and frail. I thought, "Once done, it is abuse but to repeat it becomes a habit." I now knew what had to be done.

With an attorney's counseling, I prepared the steps for a divorce. A sheriff arrived to present Jerry the papers as he had just returned from work and was having his dinner. Thereafter he'd visit his mother each night after his meal with us. After the final separation he moved back into the somber attic apartment he grew up in.

What I could not have foreseen was his mellowing when he visited his daughter every other week for a few hours. Temporarily I too lived in a somber attic apartment. During marriage I had lost my credit rating. Erika went into day care while I now worked in an advertising studio, as an art director. My self-esteem had been totally crushed. New hope surged within me now. I bought a brand new, bright yellow VW Rabbit. With the car paid off and my credit rating restored, I was now looking for a home.

Jerry wanted to come back. His mother was about to retire and now wanted to live near her son Klaus in Florida, who had a small cottage for her next to his. Habits do not change. Very shortly after her move there his happy marriage dissolved. After many years, her apparent manipulation caused these two divorces. Not long after, Jerry left for Germany. I was solely responsible for the child.

20 Connecticut-Family-Another Career c

Connecticut, Family Life – Commercial Art

BEGINNING ONCE MORE meant searching for a new base, a home. The realtor enthusiastically appraised this prospective house for a good price. It was a five-bedroom raised ranch, well maintained on a private 1/3 acre lot with an above-the-ground swimming pool, fenced and gated. I objected that my daughter and I would feel lonely; it was much too spacious. "Just a starter home, in a year or two you'll move to your dream house," the efficient Realtor replied. Just then I was fired again from my job. My work was considered very professional, but I took too much time off tending my daughter's frequent high fevers and early childhood diseases she contracted in the day care. What to do?

Already I had some client contacts, and miraculously freelance assignments started to arrive. In the beginning I had to freelance mostly in advertising studios or corporate offices.

The mortgage had been approved. Single women, rarely at this time in 1978, took on property. Erika was five years old and was happy to move into this house. She had a swing set, and in a hurry, she learned to swim to enjoy the pool. There were neighborhood friends and ample space for birthday parties and sleep-overs. We contentedly grew into this space and stayed for fourteen years until she departed for college.

Erika attended a private kindergarten, Piper's Hill, a castle-like structure on scenic grounds. In our spare time we explored the eastern states national parks, traditional New England beaches from Maine to Rhode Island to Connecticut. I joined a ski club with a spacious lodge in Vermont. Our winter weekends were then mostly preoccupied with skiing to our hearts content both in Vermont and Quebec.

Stamford, Connecticut, became headquarters for the corporate Fortune 500 in the United States. Thereafter real estate prices soared. During my stay in Stamford, I supported us freelancing from these corporate accounts. Later it was a benefit to work out of my home studio, so I was available when Erika came home from school or to attend class functions. Our living quarters were on the second level. The lower level served as workspace. The family room with fireplace as well became playroom for sleep-overs and parties. A wall had been removed in one of the bedrooms joining the family room, making it a huge L-shape space. My initial small drawing table was set up here, where I spent many evenings, nights and weekends working under deadlines. Later I set up a worktable, with ample shelving, and I acquired another large drawing table. When it was not used for table tennis, it served to store the multitude of pages preparing corporate magazines. Another space on that level became a darkroom to house a full size printer's stat camera. A client bathroom and opening to a porch and yard to do spraying made it a perfect set up.

The work was so diversified it never became tedious, with only perhaps the many hours of work on occasion. In line of graphics, first came the mechanicals, the low end of advertising. Later I worked on layouts, story boards, designs and illustrations. Some of my clients were Anaconda, Pepsi, UPS, Peabody, Polo, Litton Industries, Connecticut Art Director's Club, Xerox, Juran Institute, Aviation Safety, Pitney Bowes, Lone

Star Industries, Direct Marketing, Omega Engineering, Faber Birren, Thermatool, US Surgical, American Cystoscope, Union Carbide, St. John's Hospital, Ciba Geigi, American Can, Texas Gulf, Trintex. The geographical range extended from western Connecticut to New York.

Some of the more exciting assignments of Barbara J. Zavada Associates consisted of illustrating a search and rescue mission for Aviation Safety, producing Polo magazine, touring behind scenes and sketching polo ponies in games, designing new product lines for Pepsi, a TWA interior color design assigned by world renowned colorist Faber Birren, painting a cover for Industrial Gas, creating slide rules for Thermatool - UPS and International Aviation, scholarship graphics for Greenwich Academy.

The Publisher of Belvoir and his two vice presidents took me for lunch to a fine restaurant overlooking the Long Island Sound. Our animated talk centered around aviation. I discovered that I had more flying experience than the heads of the company producing flying magazines. They offered me a position as Art Director. Included was the use of their Cessna 180 company plane.

Producing several magazines on time with the inevitable deadlines meant many hours overtime. I still wanted to be a mother, at home for the last few years, and was doing well enough freelancing. I had another offer to fly a company plane, also a Cessna, from Glatzer Corporation. It a was tempting proposition but time was so scarce.

Though for a year I did accept a contract with Trintex, an IBM/Sears marriage. This was without training to do experimental computer advertising in color, creating on uncharted grounds. Erika had a ski accident and needed surgery. I worked a double shift to accommodate my own clients as well as to pay off her hospital bills. The end of that year I had a breakdown.

It was spring skiing at Bromley, Vermont, when Erika's ski tip got caught in the soft snow and the binding did not release. She was an excellent and fast skier. Her shriek in pain prepared me for the worst. The ski patrol brought her down by toboggan from the steep slopes. One leg had a torn ligament and crushed knee-cap. With temporary tapes and crutches I headed home for the best orthopedic surgeon for consultation. Immediately she was admitted for surgery. She was very brave and got plenty of sym-pathy and attention all around. With only a long scar for proof she again later resumed varsity sports. My insurance would not cover the cost of the doctor or hospital bill. I was in deep debt. I was not aware that one could negotiate the bill, and her father ignored the incident. She was well, that's what mattered but I ended up paying for the year to come.

Erika was surely growing up while her father had settled in Germany. He remembered her with greetings only for the holi-days. Every three to five years he would visit and spend part of an afternoon with her. After these brief visits she'd be heartbroken and cling to me and cry. It was for me to console her. She missed the father in her life. I pleaded with Jerry to give more of himself to his only daughter, but to no avail. When she was ten years old, we visited Europe. We traveled with her father to some nearby sights in Germany. We also received a warm welcome from my side of the family and some old dear friends. Then we continued on our own, exploring Switzerland, France and Holland. Those years Jerry spent his vacations with his mother, partaking in ex-otic travels in the wider expanse of Europe or visiting with her in Florida. He also connected with his nobility clan, visiting or tak-ing in holidays staying at family estates or castles. Child support payments had stopped by now.

To pass on our German speaking heritage, I enrolled Erika at the Independent German Language School, in Westport for Saturday morning classes. Of course she saw no reason to learn to speak German, as none of her friends did, and she tried to get out of these lessons. Only a few years later she surprised me, thanking me for persisting in her German classes.

Then I was offered a position of vice president from Dr. Renate Ludanyi, the founder and principal of the Independent German Language school. Life was busy but it was also rewarding for me to partake in meetings planning the school's progress. My promotional graphics were also appreciated.

From public school Erika changed over to Greenwich Academy in Greenwich, a neighboring town. After testing, she was admitted on a partial scholarship. This was the fourth oldest private girls' school in the U.S., housed in the former impressive Vanderbilt mansion. The girls wore uniforms, and teaching was by a most capable caring staff. Every immigrant's dream is to educate their children in the hope of them finding a satisfying career and a life with less hardship than they themselves had to endure. I had most yearned for a formal education. No sacrifice seemed to be too great to offer Erika this advantage. She would be the first female on both sides of the family to be earning a degree. This was my goal.

Now she took advanced German classes at the Academy. She no longer had need for the German School, so I resigned from my position as well. Dr. Ludanyi asked me to stay on and offered me the position of executive vice president. My time was getting more scarce as I now volunteered my graphics expertise for the Academy's Mother's Benefit scholarship fund. This position I held until Erika's high school graduation.

Each year, summers offered fun activities to look forward to.

Erika played varsity field hockey and lacrosse, which some summers took her to practice camps in Florida and Vermont. She also partook in private camps in Massachusetts, Maine, New Mexico, Arizona.

Sometimes I felt the burden of being alone keeping up with house chores and repairs. An extensive yard with lawn and shrubs, my demanding self employment, and tending to the needs of family, church, volunteer work and pursuing fine art. Yet it meant a busy and fulfilling life.

20 Connecticut-Family-Another Career d

Connecticut Fine Art

SOMETHING WAS MISSING. An artist needs to create. This demanding schedule of family life, plus supporting us, barely left time for me to find a way to replenish my stamina. To maintain my high level of energy we played tennis at the neighborhood courts, we bicycled the local roads or toured the coast, skied cross country on the golf courses, downhill skied in Vermont and Quebec, but on a more regular basis I walked. After assignments, sometimes late at night, I would head out in the rain or deepest snow to walk for an hour.

Once a week at night I attended sketch class, my special treat, at Silvermine School of Art in New Canaan. As a group we worked from a nude model to study anatomy, so important for the illustrator. I experimented with bamboo brush or pen and Chinese ink, with free flowing minimal strokes. Contact with fellow artists was equally stimulating.

I spent a lot of time in solitude, laboring many hours, nights and weekends in my home studio. Some of the corporate art directors I worked with became friends. It was great mental stimulation to invite them for lunch on the patio, a swim in the pool and partake in an exchange of ideas. We maintained these casual get togethers at least once a week. I'd share informa-tion gained from meetings at the New York Art Directors Club. Here too I learned about copyright laws, which were still in the forming stages in the USA. With my new acquired knowledge I was able to challenge some clients about copyrights pertaining to reproducing my art work and being remunerated for duplications and retaining originals. This was representation of VEGA, Visual Artist's and Gallery Association. I attended numerous meetings with VEGA on the upper floors of the impressive World Trade Center.

Gradually I began to take time to sketch in pen and ink and then in pastel. Some of these renderings I translated onto canvas in acrylic whenever I could snatch time. So along with my graphics I would haul along my portfolio to visit and interview galleries. Stamford Art Association was founded at this time and with it came the acquisition of a three floor town house. Now there was ample exhibition space for juried shows in all diverse media. With exposure of my abstract expressionistic canvases and garnering some awards, I was invited to join the Board of Directors. My responsibility became monitoring the life drawing class, housed in the basement. It was tight scheduling to accommodate all these demands, but it could be done. As a matter of fact the more involved I became with family and community, the more capable I felt of handling all. Each new day presented challenges and moreover joys. Life was good.

With new paintings produced I was able to continue exhibiting ever new works. Some of these solo shows included the Museum of Art Science and Industry in Bridgeport, Greenwich Museum, The Connecticut Women's Bank in Greenwich, numerous SAA group exhibits in Stamford, New Canaan Society for Arts, Landmark Tower Rotunda in Stamford, Virginia Beach Arts Festival Virginia VA, Southern Connecticut State University in New Haven, Trintex Computer Exhibit national, several juried Connecticut group exhibits at the Stamford Museum, Fennel

Gallery, Taos NM.

Juggling graphics and fine art left me thinking, where is this leading to? My passion and hard work were rewarded by seemingly insignificant rewards, a listing in the New York Artist and the American Artist. It was the boost to keep me going. At a lecture at the Larry Aldrich Museum and again at my Stamford Tower Rotunda exhibit I met Robert Motherwell, the renown abstract expressionist. With a warm handshake we had an inspiring, encouraging talk.

21 Traveling the USA and discovering the Southwest

DURING SUMMERS I had exceptionally slow work flow, but it was a time to take one's mind off the graphics business. June until August 1986, Erika and I took a camping tour of the USA for seven weeks covering 14,500 miles in the small 320i BMW. It turned out to be a most memorable journey, especially kindling love for the arid desert southwest. We covered the southern states first, briefly exploring Mexico then headed north on the west coast into Canada to visit family in Vancouver, then headed for the Canadian Rockies. We visited many national parks but the wide open spaces of the southwest desert, canyon country with its charm of Native American lore especially appealed to us.

Again a dream was born. I had a new plan to break away from a stressful life of solely maintaining a large home, and from obligations of a single parent, private school, home graphics studio and volunteering. Gradually, I had thoughts on how to make this change happen to simplify life and paint full time. Recurrent thoughts of the remote - peaceful southwest kept me holding on until my obligations were met. The goal for the exodus was set for after Erika departed for college. I would be free then. I yearned to realize my potential to create full-time.

Hard years were still ahead but I had a dream. Each summer I ventured out west to explore the Grand Canyon and many of Utah's national parks. I sketched images of Native Americans in pastel. Some I exhibited in Taos but most of those early

246

impressions were shown at much later times in museums.

My friend Alex A. turned out to be my staunchest supporter as he too was to leave Connecticut for the west. Also an immigrant, he arrived in California as a young child from Russia over the long hazardous track through Asia. The nobility were persecuted under Stalin and his family and close friends had narrow escapes. He again spent his final years where he grew up, near San Francisco.

One summer I took Erika out to central Arizona. Orme was a wilderness survival camp. The following year she was accepted for a National Science Foundation, a scholarship in a geology program of students from a cross section of the US. I drove her out to the University of Colorado in Colorado Springs. Alone, I then headed to Taos to study the masters and observe the contemporary art scene. I found a treasure of discoveries in Santa Fe, Silver City, Tucson, Bisbee, Prescott, Jerome the art colony I was to settle in later, Sedona with its church of the holy cross bedded in the red cliffs, the Grand Canyon, Coral Reef, walk in the Narrows of Zion, Bryce, Arches. I was happily satiated with desert beauty, although I had to bide my time to settle here permanently.

The economy downturn was readily recognizable by my decreasing advertising assignments during Erika's senior year. In frustration of a slower work load, I kept busy stretching canvases, starting new paintings. Then when we finished researching eastern colleges we finally mailed off applications for financial aid. Money was more scarce than ever.

We spent enjoyable holidays with Alex and California friends, the Ilian clan. It was a brief respite. Stress must have taken over as right after I became ill for a lengthy period. I felt at rock bottom, as Erika desperately needed a scholarship. There was no response from her father, his only child, who in a well off position resided in Germany. This of course was expected, since there hadn't been any child support for many years. It was not a thought to linger on. As an immigrant, I forged ahead as best I could.

Erika made Cum Laude at Greenwich Academy. Of the several colleges she applied to, Tufts University, Wellesley, her choice was the Washington University of St. Louis primarily for the full scholarship offered. It was a tearful acceptance with the thought of moving to the midwest. All her friends attended eastern colleges. Yet for her these turned out to be exciting college years.

One hurdle passed, I now prepared to dissolve my Stamford life, commencing January 1990. Some quiet evenings, while disposing of the remainder of my firewood, I sat before the comforting fireplace and sorted materials to be burned. I started sorting out the multitude of my drawings done over the past years, even some paintings and tossed them into the blaze. It was a satisfying activity, bringing me closer to my goal of desert life. Next my graphic files came under hard scrutiny. My four-drawer file cabinet was bulging and needed careful eliminations. Then came black Sunday and even before warm temperatures set in, I was forced to give up on this elimination process.

All fury broke loose. The hot water furnace, located in the garage broke resulting in a time-consuming replacement. Then the phone, lifeline to the world, took a month to properly be repaired. The faithful BMW now needed a strut replaced, the steering column and radiator looked after. Febrary 4th was black Sunday. We were invited out for the day. I shut off the kerosene heater, but apparently a miniscule spark was still flickering. Late that evening we returned to find the upper and lower level of the house with every crevice covered with a black greasy film of soot.

Walls, rugs, even the inside of cupboards, clothes closets were covered with a substance almost impossible to clean. Where to sit, where to sleep, what to wear? The homeowners insurance proved a blessing. For the longest period though, a cleaning crew came with chemicals. All had to be scrubbed down. A large number of paintings had to be taken to an art restorer in New York. It was embarrassing to be wearing the same clothes day after day to school and work. The freshly painted interior walls took a toll.

During this time Alex proved to be great support. The Harvard Club in New York City hosted a Native American dinner and panel discussion and knowing of my interest he invited me to this diversion for a great evening. He was there to calm me with, "this too shall pass." And the house did get restored again.

I kept painting to keep my sanity. Very little work or money came in. It was the beginning of the faltering economy. A first indicator was elimination of nonessential services, like graphics.

My abstract Tesuque sunset was accepted for the juried Connecticut art exhibit at the Stamford Museum. Simultaneously I was awarded a solo show at the University of Southern Connecticut in New Haven for this last summer. Also I was named finalist of the National Pen Women which proved to be my transition from commercial to fine art.

It was a time when I barely stopped for a breath. I now researched and bought a Jeep Cherokee Sport for southwest travel. Plans were made to paint the exterior of the house, myself staining the front of the house wood paneling and the rear double deck porch. With some delay even the stat camera, occupying a whole room, was sold to an upstate printer. I painted, repaired, gardened, planted shrubs, and sealed the driveway to make the house attractive to a potential renter.

Happily I prepared for Erika's graduation. At Greenwich

Academy girls graduated in a white long gown, white gloves, a bouquet of flowers. Mothers and daughters teamed for this big event. Girls got to ask the fellows at Brunswick, the adjoining school for an escort. First there was all the excitement, over which university or college everyone was accepted at, then daily news of who asked whom for a date. It was all pleasantly exhausting for the bystander, but finally all found a date. Then the Brunswick boys asked the GA girls for dates to their graduation and various formal functions. Erika needed a separate gown for these events as well. It was a time to keep a mother busily buzzing about.

At honors convocation Erika walked away with a stack of awards, same at the sports event. Her awards covered our whole dining room table. I was taken aback and almost felt embarrassed.

Dave Hate, Erika's date, looked handsome in his tuxedo, cumberbund, and pink bow tie. Like Erika, he also was to study medicine and was accepted at WestPoint. He picked Erika up for his Brunswick prom which was held on a floating boat on the Long Island Sound.

22 Freedom to Be

THE RENTAL REALTOR placed this attractive listing. "Immaculate
five-bedroom home with third of an acre well groomed yard adjoining a mumbling creek, in private area but close to downtown
Stamford and rail commute to New York." I was faced with two
offers. The Californian with a wife, twin daughters and governess
found the clean home his first choice, although his salary afford-
ed him a bigger more luxurious rental. I was concerned that with
his salary and bonuses he would not stay the full two-year term,
which I intended them to stay before opting to sell the home.
This proved to be correct. But for one year I had good tenants.

The end of summer was approaching. Erika waitressed at
"Friendly's" and had a very active and happy social life. Our furnishings and BMW went into storage and odd accumulations
were disposed of in a huge yard sale. The day arrived when Erika
departed from Kennedy Airport for St. Louis. We hugged farewell, only to meet again in a few days when I was to transport her
computer, bicycle and some other cumbersome belongings necessary for college life at University of St. Louis. My heart tugged.
How had she grown up so fast? Tears welled in my eyes as this
attractive and so self-assured young woman turned towards her
destination with a confident stride – not once looking back at her
mother. Just this fleeting moment, the thought flashed through
my mind that I had succeeded. She was prepared for life. With
an emotional outburst of tears I succumbed to Alex's supportive
embrace, the dearest friend for most of our Stamford years.

The very next day Catherine Hate, mother of Erika's friend

and prom date Dave, invited me to West Point for lunch to visit her son. It rained all day. I was informed that David would be kept in very strict isolation for his four-year stay at the academy. He did aspire to the iron man his first year, an honor of accomplishing first in sports and academics. As we toured this noble impressive old institution, we each looked for comfort in the loss of our children.

The new, gleaming white Jeep Cherokee sport was packed with the essential belongings for my southwest initiation. Alex, my dear friend, strongly insisted in my resting up for just another day. Finally the time arrived for me to bid the Alden household farewell. Then along the way I breakfasted at Bunny's, a lifelong friend in Summit, New Jersey. Nevertheless I received her blessings, but in her opinion, my relocation was a total mistake that was I getting myself into.

In western Pennsylvania I entered the beautiful hazy Skyline

Life long friend Bunny McAlpine, 1998

Drive of the Blue Ridge Parkway. For the first time peace and joy filled my heart on this freedom ride. I stopped at Washington University of St. Louis to deliver the essential college stuff to Erika. It was incredibly hot and humid on this mid August day as I met with Erika, tightly surrounded by her new friends. I felt like an intruder, but content she had acclimatized so quickly. After an impressive orientation at this gothic designed university, we dined at a Chinese restaurant of her choice. At peace I departed for the unknown.

First came the rolling green hills of Kansas. Then I briefly checked out Taos, Santa Fe, Flagstaff, and Sedona. August 17, 1990, I arrived at Dead Horse Ranch Park, Arizona, passing through a dangerously high flooded wash with my fully packed Jeep. I pitched my circular LL Bean tent then started an intensive search for housing. The welcome monsoon season brought moisture to the bone dry dessert. For the week I camped here, rains and hailstorms pelted upon the earth. Even with greater fury at nights, lightning illuminated the interior of my tent, and packs of coyotes howled uncomfortably close by. Mornings I was greeted by strangely striding roadrunners and quail scurrying about the campsite. Without much difficulty, I located an affordable one-bedroom apartment in the small, former mining town of Clarkdale, Arizona.

23 Jerome Studio

I LIVED AT the foothills of Mingus Mountain, in Verde Valley, Arizona, then had to climb the steep winding road to the mining town of Jerome. Finally I succumbed to Hank Bowen's pressured invitation to take up studio space at the old hospital, later used as Clubhouse high above the town at about 5500 ft., in the ghost town's ghostliest of buildings. It was the end of the twentieth century and I think I coped quite well fending off cold appraising Jeromite glances. I was just one more eccentric to be written into Jerome's already colorful history. I checked out the building twice - carefully - for a suitable niche among three vast, dusty, crumbling, high ceilinged floors. On the second floor, the southwest corner room allowed privacy, a door with lock and off to the northwest another room for storage. The windows were magnificent. They were tall with intricate laid out glass panels, although now mostly broken, allowing cool early fall breezes to sweep in gently, and at other times the wind with a low haunted haul carrying - disorganizing anything in its path. There were moments when I had to hold on to my drawings not to have them swept, pastels face down, in a fury about the dusty floor.

Hank made occasional curious visits to see what this artist was up to, philosophizing that for an artist to create one must suffer. At this stage I had hoped that my suffering, all of it, was well past. The view is awesomely inspiring. One looks into the wide expanse of Verde Valley beyond, as Sedona's red rocks gleam in the sunset bright with hues of deep blues, misty greens, shocking pinks, and sunset yellows in the sky. The San Francisco

Mountains finish off this palate of dreamlike panorama in hazy silver. Yes, it was this view that sold me this incredibly neglected, dusty, windy, steadily getting colder studio.

With a thermos of hot herbal tea and sketch pads, I ascend to the second floor, having let myself in through the front door and a combination lock on chain fitted through a broken window. I search for the northeast corner, a sunny alcove, warm during the late morning and noon hours. In the afternoon I migrate where the sun brings light and life to the study area. By 4 PM it gets chilly when the sun begins to set. I pack up hurriedly before it gets too dark to read the combination lock to let myself out, apprehensive about having to spend the night with fabled ghosts.

Right from the start the drawings take shape, form, color, mystical meaning, and I am off to an ever increasing excitement to create. I hardly feel the cold slowly crippling my fingers, or the wind blowing into my face or the low of my back. Weighting down the drawings, I work sometimes feverishly to hold on to moments of inspiration, to grasp the overabundant ideas. I want to work faster but the perfectionist I am must take the time each drawing demands. Life is exhilarating. I just want to float on this wave of creative lust, hold on to each and every inspiration. The southwest has given me this new lease on life after years of drudgery, deadlines and dead beat clients. I rejoice. Almost magically pen - brush - pastel glide over the paper laying down firm the beginning of a new creation - a drawing.

24 Freedom to Create

NOT ONLY A creative but also a delightful social period evolved. I joined the Sedona Art Association, flew with the 99ers on missions, and joined a hiking group. I got introduced to the back country wilderness by locals. I traveled extensively in the national parks in the tri-state area. I sketched hundreds of pastel drawings from these first impressions of a new land. Almost immediately I started exhibiting in galleries and museums in this early period of my arrival.

After two years I had adjusted comfortably in my new world. The Stamford residence was sold after a difficult second tenant, who nearly demolished the house. Researching Arizona, New Mexico and Utah, I found a location I could happily consider home. This was a pristine desert valley in isolation, surrounded by tall bright red cliffs close to the Colorado River, in view of the La Sal Mountains most of the year snow covered peaks. The nearest towns were on desert roads one and two hour distant travels.

My view of red cliff canyons

How I learned to love the sound of the southwest wind. It was a low, howling, melodic song sweeping and cutting over the plains into my heart. At last I am here. The umbilical cord was severed to the high-powered world. How I love the wide sweeping plains with an open sky, desolate desert, the red rocks, plant life, and the abundance of wildflowers in season. Most of all I am humbled by the majestic sun rises, the brilliant sunsets, the desert cool moonlit valleys.

Over a prolonged time I converted the small pink, stucco house into a working studio with privacy of acres in natural vegetation blending in with the canyons. Now I was at peace, not concerned about promotion and exhibiting, just producing the best I had to offer from my vast experiences of my European background and living in the eastern United States a life span of working and exposure in the arts. This all served in culmination for the freedom to create from my heart.

The encore to a fulfilling life was now realized by Erika's forthcoming marriage to her-long time friend John Schaefer. The wedding was to be in St. Louis, Missouri, May 16, 1998.

CPSIA information can be obtained at www.ICGtesting.com
Printed in the USA
BVOW071152300912

301736BV00003B/1/P